Stephan Elliott (r) with producer Al Clark

STEPHAN ELLIOTT's first film *Frauds* was shown in competition at the Cannes Film Festival in 1993 and his second *The Adventures of Priscilla, Queen of the Desert* was also an official selection as a special midnight screening at Cannes in 1994.

In 1991 he directed two narrative shorts, *Fast* and *The Agreement* for Latent Image, the company which subsequently developed and produced his feature films. *Frauds* was produced by Andrena Finlay and Stuart Quin, and *The Adventures of Priscilla, Queen of the Desert* by Al Clark and Michael Hamlyn. Rebel Penfold-Russell was the executive producer of both films.

THE ADVENTURES OF

Priscilla

QUEEN OF THE DESERT

Original Screenplay by

STEPHAN ELLIOTT

CURRENCY PRESS • SYDNEY

First published in 1994 by
Currency Press Ltd
PO Box 452, Paddington NSW 2021, Australia

National Library of Australia
Cataloguing-in-Publication data

    Elliott, Stephan.
       The adventures of Priscilla queen of the desert.

      ISBN 0 86819 416 6

      1. Title. II. Title: Adventures of Priscilla queen of the desert (Motion
             picture). (Series: Currency film scripts).

A822.3

Printed by Southwood Press, Marrickville, NSW
Cover design by The Master Typographer
Stills photography by Elise Lockwood.

Publisher's note: this is the reading script and includes only those camera directions which are essential to the story.

Contents

Dedicated to all the inspirationally trashy drag queens
who never turned up to the casting sessions.

From the Writer/Director

Stephan Elliott

In 1990 I wrote my first screenplay, *Frauds* which was about as much fun as giving birth to a giraffe. The truth of the matter is this: I cannot spell and the prose flows from my mouth like Waterford Crystal out of a meat grinder.

But, being incapable of backing down on a dare, and with the aid of a very cheap secretary, I climbed over the hurdle of illiteracy and stumbled across the finishing line. And the weight lifted from my shoulders. My God ... I could write!

Whilst trying to get *Frauds* off the ground, its producer Andrena Finlay quizzed me about any low-budget ideas I might have floating around in my head. Two days earlier, I'd witnessed a plume of feathers break from a drag queen's head-dress during a Mardi Gras parade and go tumbling down a deserted street like a tumbleweed from a Sergio Leone Western.

... drag queens in the outback!

After lingering over the image for a few weeks (*the* most important phase of script writing), I sat before my first computer (two fingers, and to this day, still only two fingers), and ten days later *Priscilla* was born. One minor rewrite before rehearsal and another during rehearsal, and from then on the beast grew her own stiletto and began to walk by herself. It was without doubt the most enjoyable experience of my life.

Just about every day people tell me of the great manuscript they are about to write, but it's just not quite ready yet; the government grant hasn't come through; the timing just isn't right at the moment. The lesson I have learned is simple. If you have a script floating around in your head -- just *write* the thing. You might be in for a pleasant surprise.

London, August 1994

CAST

Terence Stamp	BERNADETTE
Hugo Weaving	TICK/MITZI
Guy Pearce	ADAM/FELICIA
Bill Hunter	BOB
Sarah Chadwick	MARION
Mark Holmes	BENJAMIN
Julia Cortez	CYNTHIA
Ken Radley	FRANK
Alan Dargin	ABORIGINAL MAN
Rebel Russell	LOGOWOMAN

Executive Producer, Rebel Penfold-Russell
Produced by Al Clark and Michael Hamlyn
Written and directed by Stephan Elliott

Complete film credits appear at the end of the book.

PRINCIPAL CHARACTERS

BERNADETTE, a fifty-ish transsexual who works as a singer/dancer
TICK, in his thirties, a drag queen who performs under the name of Mitzi
ADAM, in his twenties, a drag queen who performs as Felicia
BOB, late forties, owner of an outback service station
CYNTHIA, his wife. A former dancer from Manila.
MARION, Tick's wife
BENJAMIN, Tick and Marion's eight-year-old son

1. INT. HOTEL — NIGHT

A lone female figure waits attentively in the only strip of light being emitted from the stringy curtain flimsily protecting her from the huge crowd gathered on the other side. With a musical 'intro', she takes three deep breaths and flings the curtain to one side.

ROLL CREDITS . . .

A fierce spotlight hits front on, backlighting her massive head of blonde hair and sparkling sequinned dress. The music drowns the wild applause of the crowd. She then begins to belt out a familiar song, Charlene's 'I've Never Been To Me'. This is MITZI, *the showgirl, and she sings on a make-shift stage assembled behind the bar of a very popular city pub.*

 The mob is singing along now. MITZI *is building for the climax of the number. She spreads her legs wide and raises her arms, finishing off with all the energy she can muster.*

 The crowd goes wild. People are crammed around the bar, smashing their beer cans up and down and screaming for more. MITZI *is exhausted. She smiles and waits for the commotion to die down. It doesn't. More! More! Insults are traded with gay abandon. Encore! Encore! No. She waves goodbyes and attempts to move off stage, much to the dismay of the crowd. They stamp their feet and begin to scream.* MITZI *turns and looks across the sea of young, angry, drunken faces. It is not a very attractive sight. She resumes her exit, and moves back to the curtain, only to be hit on the back of the head by an empty beer can. She falls forward to the floor, more in shock than pain. Another pair of heels click swiftly to her aid. It is* FELICIA, *a fellow performer.*

FELICIA: Are you OK?
MITZI: Yeah.
 MITZI moves into the dressing room, leaving FELICIA to a crowd of ferocious hecklers.
FELICIA: Oh, well that was fucking charming, you gutless pack of dick heads!
HECKLER: Oh fuck off, you talentless dog!
FELICIA: What was that?
HECKLER: Show us your pink bits.
FELICIA: No, I don't think I will. Now do you know why this microphone has such a long cord? So it's easily retrieved

after I've shoved it up your arse!

The crowd roar with laughter as another music cue begins.

2. INT. HOTEL DRESSING ROOM/TICK'S BEDROOM — NIGHT

MITZI is staring at her horrible reflection in the mirror. Her face make-up is totally over the top, her eyelashes are long and beaded, her lipstick is smeared. Lifting her hand from her now bruised jaw, she grabs a clump of her hair and pulls. The wig falls by the wayside. Underneath is a man. TICK BELROSE is an unhappy drag queen. FELICIA storms back into the dressing room, and by the tone of her furious voice, we realise that she too is a man.

FELICIA: What the fuck's going on out there tonight? Are you hurt?

TICK waves her off with a flop of the hand. FELICIA turns to the other sneering drag queens in the dressing room.

All right, which one of you bitches shat on my dress?

They all shriek with laughter. A very glamorous telephone is dumped on the table in front of TICK.

VOICE: [*off*] Tick, it's for you . . .

TICK collects the phone very unenthusiastically.

TICK: Hello?

WOMAN's VOICE: [*off*] Ding dong! Avon calling. Howdy sunshine. Long time no hear.

INTERCUT WITH . . .

3. INT. HOSPITAL CORRIDOR FLASHBACK — DAY

A DOCTOR rips the surgical mask from his face and hands it to the NURSE walking attentively alongside.

DOCTOR: Where?

NURSE: Emergency Ward A.

The DOCTOR turns into a corridor and confidently throws open the two large swinging doors in front of him. His stride is suddenly cut short with the sight before him. MITZI (TICK), done up in spectacular drag.

DOCTOR: Mr Belrose?
MITZI (TICK): [*nervously*] Yes?

4. INT. HOTEL DRESSING ROOM — NIGHT

WOMAN's VOICE: [*off*] So? How about it?
TICK is listening to the voice on the telephone in silence. He lowers his eyes down to the oversized diamond ring on one of his fingers.

5. EXT. DIRTY INNER-CITY STREET — NIGHT

TICK is making his way down a very unattractive street in the rain. He is a very 'normal' looking 31-year-old; quite tall and handsome. Fights are going on, but he is blind to it all. He passes a telephone and suddenly stops. Then, reaching for a coin, he gets inside and dials.

INTERCUT WITH . . .

6. INT. BERNADETTE'S APARTMENT — NIGHT

Not much can be seen. Only the telephone ringing on the sideboard. Eventually a hand reaches over and lifts the receiver.

BERNADETTE: [*off, crying*] Yeah.
TICK: Bernadette, it's Tick. Sorry to call you so late, but I . . . [*hearing the tears*] Hey! Are you ok?
The voice offscreen is giving way to the tears.
BERNADETTE: [*off*] No I'm not.
TICK: What's the matter?
BERNADETTE:[*off*] Trumpet just died.

7. EXT. CEMETERY — DAY

A large city cemetery. A handful of young men and sobbing drag queens dressed in very fashionable black, surround a casket with a trumpet resting on top. TICK glances from the PRIEST in mid-prayer to apparently the only woman in the group: BERNADETTE. She is a fifty-year-old transsexual, very well dressed, but overly made up; and the tears have forced their way through the heavy mascara, leaving blackened trails on the cheeks behind them.

WITH THE FUNERAL COMPLETE . . .

BERNADETTE and TICK walk briskly through the cemetery.

BERNADETTE: It's not fair. I've spent half my life and all my savings trying to snag a sympathetic husband. The selfish little shit goes and dies on me.

TICK: Twenty-five years old and he slips over in a bathroom.

BERNADETTE: He didn't slip. He was peroxiding his hair at home again and he asphyxiated on the fumes.
She struggles to hold back the tears. Eventually . . .

TICK: I've got to get some space. I've been offered a job out of town . . .

BERNADETTE: That's nice.

TICK: Why don't you come with me? I need some help and I think we could both use the break.

BERNADETTE: You're not wrong. Where is it?

TICK: Alice Springs.
BERNADETTE stops and looks after TICK. He is deadly serious.

BERNADETTE: You've got to be fucking joking.

8. INT. TICK'S APARTMENT — NIGHT

Deep in the bowels of the hotel, hidden behind hundreds of flamboyant frocks, is a small bed and living area. Photos litter the walls, wigs of every shape and colour are spread across the bedhead. It is all very disorganised. TICK is seated before a gaudy arrangement of facial products and a completely impressionable potential customer.

TICK: 'Wo-Man' is a unique range of speciality facial products designed for the more . . . heavy duty woman in all of us. Now this week . . .
The phone alongside rings.
Excuse me.

INTERCUT WITH . . .

9. INT. BERNADETTE'S APARTMENT — NIGHT

BERNADETTE, phone in hand, a map of Australia in the other, struggles to retain the tears.

BERNADETTE: How long is the run?
 TICK smiles.
TICK: Four weeks. Equity minimum, two shows a night, accommodation included.
 After a moment of deliberation . . .
BERNADETTE: I can't just sit around here crying all the time. [*Looking in the mirror*] Jesus. My mascara keeps running. I look like a raccoon.
TICK: Good girl. That's the spirit.
BERNADETTE: Here's hoping the desert is big enough for the two of us ...
TICK: Three of us.

10. INT. TICK'S APARTMENT — DAY

ADAM WHITELY, also known as FELICIA, comes steaming into the room, his arms laden with frocks. He is a handsome twenty-four-year-old totally over-the-top Sydney 'scene queen'.

ADAM: [*singing*]
 A desert holiday
 Let's pack the drag away.
 You take the lunch and tea.
 I'll take the ecstasy.
 Fuck off you silly queer,
 I'm getting out of here.
 A desert holiday.
 Hip, hip, hip, hip hurray!
  He has floated out of the room already. TICK looks over to BERNADETTE, whose face is one of absolute horror. With ADAM out of earshot . . .
BERNADETTE: Why?
TICK: Why not? Look, he's turned into a bloody good little performer.
BERNADETTE: [*getting angry*] That's right. A bloody good little

performer. Twenty-four hours a day, seven days a week. I thought we were getting away from all this shit!

ADAM: Two's a company, three's a party, Bernadette my sweet.

He struts triumphantly back into the room. BERNADETTE *turns.*

BERNADETTE: [*cynically*] We're unplugging our curling wands and going bush, Felicia. Why would you possibly want to leave all this glamour for a hike into the middle of nowhere?

ADAM: Do you really want to know?

BERNADETTE: Desperately.

ADAM: Ever since I was a lad, I've had a dream . . . a dream that I now finally have a chance to fulfil.

BERNADETTE: And that is?

ADAM: [*pausing for effect*] To travel to the centre of Australia, to climb Kings Canyon as a queen, in a full-length Gautier sequin, heels and tiara.

ADAM floats across the room. BERNADETTE *looks up to* TICK *in disgust.*

BERNADETTE: Great. That's just what this country needs. A cock in a frock on a rock.

TICK: Oh, get back in your kennels, both of you. Now the first thing we have to work out is how the hell we're going to get there.

11. EXT. CITY STREET — DAY

ADAM climbs down the steps of a rickety old silver bus. The old beast has been passed on from backpacker to backpacker over the years, and the pile of spare tyres along with the large water tank on the roof suggest it has seen some rugged terrain. TICK, *and particularly* BERNADETTE, *stare in disbelief.*

ADAM: Tah-da! What do you think?

TICK: When do we have to return it to the school?

ADAM: We don't. We own it.

TICK: What?

ADAM: I met some nice Swedish tourists called Lars, Lars and Lars, and coaxed it out of them for 10,000 bucks!

BERNADETTE: We can't afford it!

ADAM: Well, that's right.

> ADAM *reaches into the front of the bus and retrieves a bottle of champagne. Then, donning a very childish voice . . .*

ADAM: Mummy . . . Maybe a trip to the outback would help me get over this little phase I'm going through. You never know, I might meet some lonely country girl!

> ADAM *raises the bottle above his head.*

I hereby christen this budget barbie camper . . . 'Priscilla! Queen of the Desert!'

> *The bottle explodes.*

BERNADETTE: That's got to be the understatement of the century.

MONTAGE MUSIC BEGINS

12. INT. TICK'S APARTMENT/MONTAGE — DAY

MUSIC CARRIES OVER

TICK, *out of all three, is going to have the most trouble. He owns more frocks than his two companions put together. He opens a rather large bag and stuffs in a massive Spanish gown filled with hoops. Into the next bag goes the entire range of 'Wo-Man' facial products and the pyramid selling handbook.*

CUT TO . . .

13. INT. BERNADETTE'S APARTMENT/MONTAGE — NIGHT

BERNADETTE *is a little bit more controlled. Her performance frocks take up a few bags, her casual clothes a couple of others . . . but her shoe collection is enormous!*

CUT TO . . .

14. INT. ADAM'S APARTMENT/MONTAGE

Alongside ADAM *stands his sympathetic* MOTHER, *an over-dressed try-hard Eastern suburbs art dealer, who is busily pulling frocks out and sizing them up against her son. 'Yes dear, that's a nice one'. ADAM's face says it all.*

15. EXT. CITY STREET/HOTEL — DAY

MUSIC CARRIES OVER

A small contingent of OFFICIALS politely applaud beneath a painted banner which reads 'Coast to Coast Classic'. A lone woman, completely covered in the sponsor's logos (LOGOWOMAN) is strapping a supply buggy to her waist in preparation for her epic jog across the continent. The mood is very serious and subdued.

In contrast, 'Priscilla' is parked in front of a large inner city hotel. A crowd of screeching gay well-wishers have gathered, all waving balloons and streamers. BERNADETTE is blowing kisses from the driver's window. ADAM is hanging out of the back safety window with TICK, who is throwing samples to the crowd.

BERNADETTE: Ladies, start your engines!
> *As 'Priscilla' pulls out from the curb, we see her roof crowded high with luggage. Behind, LOGOWOMAN along the road, pulling her buggy behind.*

MUSIC FADES OUT

16. EXT/INT. LUSH COUNTRYSIDE — DAY

'Priscilla' purrs her way through some very fertile plains. From inside the bus, we can hear singing . . .

INSIDE THE BUS . . .

17. INT. BUS — DAY

BERNADETTE is behind the wheel leading the happy threesome through a singalong. ADAM and TICK are crowded in behind, their faces flushed with excitement. What adventure! This first glimpse of the bus interior is very unusual. The seats have been replaced with a handful of camp beds and old lounge suites. Metres of coloured sash have been strung down the length of the sides above the windows. At the back is a small kitchenette crowded with masses of fairy lights.

LAP DISSOLVE

18. INT. BUS — DAY

ADAM is behind the wheel now. BERNADETTE has moved a short distance down the aisle. TICK is looking at a road map. Enthusiasm is dying rapidly.

LAP DISSOLVE

19. INT. BUS — DAY

TICK is driving. BERNADETTE and ADAM are sitting at the back of the bus quite exhausted. The song is now a whisper. ADAM lets out a sigh.

ADAM: How long have we been on the road?
BERNADETTE: Four and a half hours.
ADAM: Christ, I've got a splitting headache already.
　　ADAM moves to the kitchenette which has had quite a few customised adjustments made to it. A large mirror adorned by make-up lights has been suspended from one wall. A rack has been assembled to hang the delicate frocks. ADAM opens the large First Aid kit fastened to a seat revealing the arsenal of alcohol — gin, vodka and scotch bottles stacked two deep.
ADAM: Happy hour!
BERNADETTE: Mother's ruin *pour moi*!
TICK: Long Island Tea.
ADAM: And a Stoly and tonic for me!

20. EXT/INT. COUNTRY PLAINS — DUSK

The vegetation is changing. The greens are giving way to harsh browns and yellows. A cloud of dust is following 'Priscilla'.

21. INT. BUS — DAY

TICK is sewing sequins onto a dress. ADAM has poured himself a stiff vodka and tonic. They sit facing each other deep in conversation.

TICK: Well, listen to this one. After we did the Abba show, Kevin had one of those liposuction penis enlargements.

ADAM: He didn't!

TICK: You know what they do? They siphon all the fat out of your love handles and actually inject it into your wing wang.

ADAM: Yucky tuu. I suppose it gives a whole new meaning to 'cracking a fat' though, doesn't it?

They bray with laughter. BERNADETTE, behind the wheel, finally cracks.

BERNADETTE: Oh, listen to yourselves. You sound like two fat slags at a pie bake-off.

Stunned silence.

ADAM: Your contribution to the conversation hasn't exactly made headlines, Bernice.

BERNADETTE: Gee, poor Kevin's dick. There can't be much room there now, what with his brain taking up so much space already. No, I'll join this conversation on the proviso that we stop bitching about people, talking about wigs, dresses, bust sizes, penises, frugs, night clubs and bloody Abba.

Absolute silence from the back of the bus. Then . . .

TICK: Doesn't give us much to talk about, does it?

Silence. ADAM moves in toward TICK and whispers.

ADAM: Can you confirm a rumour for me . . . Is it true that her real name is Ralph?

TICK raises his finger to his mouth, desperate to shut ADAM up. He looks to the driver. No, she didn't hear. Thank God.

22. INT/EXT. ROADSIDE — NIGHT

'Priscilla' has been parked in a roadside picnic area. ADAM is busily toasting baby sausages.

ADAM: How do you like your little boys, girls?

Silence.
You don't have to answer that if you don't want to.

INTERCUT WITH INSIDE OF BUS

TICK is getting ready to bunk down in one of the camp beds. BERNADETTE has a thick white face-pack on, with cucumber slices over the eyes.

BERNADETTE: Oh my God. What is this? Outback with Benny Hill?

TICK: Just leave mine outside the door at about 8 a.m., along with an orange juice and toast, please.
ADAM carries a plate of sausages to the closed bus door and attempts to open it.

ADAM: Certainly, Madame. And would you like vegemite or jam with that?
The door won't open. ADAM struggles with the plate. The door has been locked.

ADAM: Ah, knock, knock. Room service.

TICK: Can't you read the sign? Do not disturb! Please come back in the morning.

ADAM: Oh, ha ha girls. Open the door.
TICK smiles as he climbs into his bunk.

TICK: Goodnight Bernice.

BERNADETTE: Goodnight Mitzi.

ADAM: Open the door. [*Silence.*] Open the fucking door!
Nothing. Nothing but some fake snoring.

ADAM: Okay. If you don't open the door . . . I'm going to sing.
Silence.
Fine. You asked for it. [*Singing*] 'I don't care if the sun don't shine . . .'
ADAM really belts it out. The longer he sings, the louder he gets. He circles the bus, pounding on the windows. BERNADETTE and TICK cover their heads with their pillows.

TICK: Night, John Boy.

LIGHTS OUT

23. EXT. DEEP COUNTRY — DAY

The earth all around is turning yellow and crusty. The trees have given way to clumps of dense bush. 'Priscilla' rumbles by.

INSIDE THE BUS

24. INT. BUS — DAY

ADAM is driving. There are big bags under his eyes.

ADAM: I'm seriously falling asleep.
 BERNADETTE is behind him reading a magazine.
BERNADETTE: No. It's your shift and you're going to stick to it. Serves you right for staying out all night. Slut.
ADAM: Well, I'm not going to make it.
BERNADETTE: 'I don't care if the sun don't shine.'
TICK: Oh, fuck off, grandma.
 TICK is looking out of a window, slowly twisting the diamond ring around his finger.
BERNADETTE: Are you all right?
TICK: I'm fine. I'm just thinking.
 BERNADETTE smiles and leaves him. Finally she seats herself on the chair before the mirror. She purses her lips and checks her foundation. Unknown to her, ADAM is watching in the rear vision mirror. She takes her lipstick and unscrews the head. She slowly lines it up to her face. ADAM has a wicked look in his eyes. His foot touches the brake. Clunk. A tiny bump.
 BERNADETTE freezes. She nearly smeared herself. She tries again. Clunk. Another small bump. This time BERNADETTE waits until the road is perfectly smooth. ADAM is on stand-by. Slowly the lipstick rises up to the face, just touches the skin and . . . SLAM! ADAM hits the brake. BERNADETTE's head slops sideways, smearing a great red stripe right across her face.
ADAM: Sorry.
 ADAM sniggers to himself, looks down from the rear vision mirror and is caught totally by surprise.
 Shit.
 He begins to decelerate.

TICK: What is it?

25. EXT. SCRUBBY HILL — DAY

ADAM brings the bus to a standstill on top of a semi-grassy hill. The doors open and the three occupants climb down onto the bitumen. Their faces are a mixture of awe, amazement and fear. After a few moments of silence . . .

ADAM: Perhaps we should have flown.

CUT TO . . .

Starting at their feet and stretching right across a vast desert all the way to the horizon is one perfectly straight road. The scope is breathtaking. None of them were expecting this. ADAM takes a few steps forward and stops.

26. EXT. DESERT — DUSK

A Mack truck road-train thunders past 'Priscilla', leaving her gasping in a tail of suffocating dust. The Fun Bus is a tiny speck on this vast highway.

27. INT. BUS — DUSK

The time is crawling by very slowly. An enthusiastic BERNADETTE is in the driver's seat, leading her companions in a game of 'I Spy'. She is taking it very seriously. ADAM is sending her up mercilessly.

ADAM: Witchetty grub. Your turn.
BERNADETTE: I spy with my little eye, something beginning with 'R'.
ADAM: Rectum.
BERNADETTE: No.
ADAM: Ring pilot.
BERNADETTE: No.
TICK: Road.

BERNADETTE: All right. What's the matter with you?

TICK: Nothing, darling.

BERNADETTE: Don't darling me, darling. Look at you. You've got a face like a cat's arse. Come on. Fess up.

TICK finds himself cornered. He shrugs his shoulders.

TICK: I'm just worried about the show, that's all. Like, we haven't done any rehearsals yet, and ...

BERNADETTE: We've got two weeks, for Christ's sake. That's plenty of time to rehearse. Now, what's your problem?

TICK: It's not a problem . . . I just want this show to be good. That's all. It's got to be good.

ADAM: How the fuck did you get this job, Mitzi, my darling? I mean who is the fish who runs this bloody hotel in the middle of nowhere anyway? Your mother?

TICK: No. My wife.

ADAM: What? Don't tell me you've got an ex-boyfriend tucked away out here somewhere.

TICK: No, my wife. I'm married.

28. EXT. BUS — DUSK

BERNADETTE hits the brakes in shock, bringing the bus to a very noisy, smoke filled and burnt rubber standstill. The sound of falling bottles eventually subsides.

29. INT. CHURCH ALTAR, FLASHBACK — DAY

A beautifully manicured hand stems from the sleeves of a perfectly white bridal dress. One expectant finger is poised before a groom's shaking hand which holds forward a wedding ring nervously. We finally see the bride and groom. A large and gleeful looking woman is dressed in a lovely set of tails and black tie. This is MARION, the groom. Standing to her right is the bride, TICK, frocked in a truly stunning wedding dress.

30. EXT. DESERT — NIGHT

The bus is on the side of the road in a sea of darkness, the only illumination being the roaring campfire. TICK lifts the diamond ring up for a silenced BERNADETTE to see. ADAM gets to his feet.

TICK: And when the joint bank account ran dry after a couple of years, I guess I preferred her wedding ring to mine. So, no drama. We swapped and called it a day.

ADAM: This is getting too weird. You . . . and a woman. What did she used to do for kicks? Put a bucket over your head and swing off the handle?

TICK: You know there are two things I don't like about you, Felicia . . . Your face. So how about shutting both of them!

ADAM: Well, at least this explains your abysmal batting average as Mitz. I often wondered why your dance card is so empty. I take it you never got a divorce.

TICK falls silent.

Well, girls, what can I say? Here's to a secret very well kept.

BERNADETTE: [*to ADAM*] Shame it's not going to stay that way, isn't it?

ADAM: Mm. Got any more little surprises you'd like to share with us? Haven't got any kids stashed away out there as well, have you?

ADAM goes, leaving the others in silence. Eventually ....

TICK: Look, I haven't lied about anything. After six years I get a phone call out of nowhere screaming for help and Christ knows I owe her a couple of favours. [*Beginning to cry*] I'm sorry that I never told you. I'm not sorry that you're here.

BERNADETTE pulls the blanket up around her shoulders and slowly walks over to TICK, giving him a gentle kiss on the head.

BERNADETTE: Don't worry about it, dolls. I'm as jealous as hell.

She leaves TICK staring into the fire and wanders quietly towards the bus.

FADE OUT

31. EXT. DESERT — MORNING

'Priscilla' tears across the plain on her epic journey west.

INSIDE

32. INT. BUS — MORNING

TICK is deep in concentration, his face straining over his hand of cards. He looks up to find his partner still sporting an idiot's grin. Finally . . .

TICK: What?

ADAM: So, was it a big wedding? Get lots of pressies, did you? I just wish I was *old* enough to have been there.

TICK: Oh, ha ha.

ADAM: I would have bought you a lovely matching set of 'hers and hers' bath mats.

TICK: Give it a rest.

ADAM: Not on your life. Imagine! Mitzi the Magnificent and her Blushing Bride! Mowing those lawns must have been murder on your heels, though.

TICK: All right, Felicia, that's enough. Let's put some money in that seething cesspool mouth of yours. If I win this game, you will never mention my wife, ever, in my presence again, OK?

ADAM: And if I win?

TICK: Name your price.

ADAM: Well now. What would I really like more than anything in the world?
    Suddenly . . .

TICK: Snap!
    TICK slams his hand down on the cards.
    Better be quick.

33. EXT. BROKEN HILL — DAY

'Priscilla' rumbles into the mining city of Broken Hill in deep inland New South Wales. It is hot and dry. The footpaths are sprinkled with well-worn country folk. Eventually, the bus pulls up noisily on the main street. Slowly, the doors open.
    An exaggerated set of stilletoed 'thongs' step out onto the

road. MITZI *emerges in a dress consisting entirely of matched things and with a very stylish beehive wig. The face paint is thick.* BERNADETTE *is dressed a little more downmarket. She is not playing this game, but in some respects she has no choice. Last to emerge is the totally mind blowing* FELICIA, *decked out in full feathers and boa.*

The townspeople come to a complete standstill. MITZI *looks back to* FELICIA.

MITZI: What the fuck am I doing? Take the bloody frock off, Felicia. Don't make it worse than it is.

FELICIA: Think I'll let you get all the attention? No chance. Come on, girls, let's go shopping!

BERNADETTE: For Christ's sake . . .

34. EXT. BROKEN HILL MONTAGE — DAY

The girls are walking down the main street. FELICIA *is being very vocal, pointing in shop windows and gasping at the horrible fashions.* MITZI *is playing it low key, but once she's in drag, the mannerisms come naturally. She flicks her hair and wobbles her bottom.* BERNADETTE *is walking ahead, trying to be very grown up about the whole thing. People are steering a very wide path around them. Once the drags have passed, they stop dead in their tracks and stare back in complete disbelief. Even a dog does so.*

Broken Hill has three drag queens walking down the street, and they are leaving a trail of confusion behind them.

35. INT. BROKEN HILL HOTEL — DUSK

MONTAGE

The three ladies stand in the foyer of the most garishly painted hotel in the world. The walls are covered with hand painted Botticelli reproductions. The corners are filled with stuffed animals. The overdressed drag queens look mild by comparison.

BERNADETTE: You've got to be kidding.

A small ageing PROPRIETOR *greets them in the hall.* MITZI, BERNADETTE *and* FELICIA *are all standing before him, smiling very politely.*

PROPRIETOR: Welcome to Mario's Palace. Come in. What can I do for you? Would you like a room, Madam?

The PROPRIETOR *is absolutely charming.*

36. INT. BROKEN HILL HOTEL ROOM — NIGHT

BERNADETTE *dumps her bag on the pretend-plush bed.* MITZI *and* FELICIA *follow suit. It is a very strange hotel room. More hand paintings — Aboriginal scenes, all over the walls.*

MITZI: Oh Tackorama! Who the hell does all the painting around here?

BERNADETTE: Someone with no arms or right foot by the look of things.

FELICIA *looks at an Aboriginal Jesus mounted on the wall.*

FELICIA: For goodness' sake, get down off that crucifix. Someone needs the wood.

MITZI *opens the mini-refrigerator.*

MITZI: What fun. Baby bottles of booze!

BERNADETTE *turns to the fridge and smiles. She takes herself a glass and opens a bottle of gin.*

BERNADETTE: Gather round, girls, I'll show you a trick. You drink the gin . . . [*She sculls the gin*] fill the empty bottle up with water, and put it back in the fridge.

MITZI: *Va t'en vous.* What about the scotch?

BERNADETTE: That's where the complimentary tea bags come in handy.

MITZI: Very clever.

Each settles into a corner with a drink in hand.

FELICIA: Cheers girls . . . And congratulations, Mitzi darling. You did it. One lap of the Broken Hill main drag in drag! That'll teach you to take on the Fairmont Boys School 'Snap' champion.

BERNADETTE: Here's to being off that fucking bus.

ALL: Chookers!

They all raise their glasses. Then, silence.

FELICIA: So, all dolled up with nowhere to go.

BERNADETTE: Well, I sure as shit have no intention of sitting in here for the rest of the evening.

> *They all look from one to another. The smiles emerge.*

FELICIA: I'm in.

> *They both look toward* MITZI, *who has an inkling of reservation in her eyes. Then . . .*

MITZI: Oh, all right. Here's hoping they have a decent cocktail bar.

37. INT. BROKEN HILL HOTEL BAR — NIGHT

The indestructible public bar is jam packed with burly miners. There is only a small handful of women present. The soft background music is only adding to the noise, which is bordering on the deafening. It all sounds like great fun. Suddenly, the uproar begins to drop off. People stare back towards the entrance of the bar. So begins a chain reaction which culminates in total silence. All heads are looking back.

> MITZI, BERNADETTE *and* FELICIA *stand at the saloon doors in full drag. After a moment, they slowly make their way toward the bar. Patrons on the stools in front clear a space. Nobody says a word. The three ladies hold their heads proudly in the air.* BERNADETTE *leans toward the* BARTENDER.

BERNADETTE: [*very feminine*] Hello. Could I have a gin and tonic, a Bloody Mary and a Lime Daiquiri please.

> *The Bartender cannot move a muscle. And suddenly, the silence is broken. A squat, rugged woman moves toward them. It is* SHIRLEY, *and she's as mean as dish water.*

SHIRLEY: Well, look what the cat dragged in! What do we have here then? A couple of showgirls, eh? Where did you ladies just come in from, Uranus?

> MITZI *drops her head. There is going to be trouble.* BERNADETTE, *who appears to be the centre of the attack, chooses to ignore* SHIRLEY.

BERNADETTE: Could I please have a . . .

> SHIRLEY *pushes forward and grabs* BERNADETTE *by the wrist in a very aggressive manner.*

SHIRLEY: No, you can't have nothing! We got nothing here for people like you. Nothing!

> BERNADETTE *is staring at* SHIRLEY'S *dirt encrusted hand*

*with eyes like saucers. The crowd is silent. They are
expecting the worst. BERNADETTE slowly peels off the
paw with equal force and turns.*

BERNADETTE: Now listen here, you mullet . . . Why don't you
just light your tampon and blow your box apart, because
it's the only bang you're ever going to get, sweetheart.

*SHIRLEY is caught completely off guard. Suddenly, an
enormous FAT MINER standing right beside her bursts
into laughter. And the bar explodes! Everybody is
falling about in stitches! SHIRLEY looks desperately from
side to side in search of support. And she isn't getting
any.*

38. INT. BROKEN HILL HOTEL BAR — NIGHT

*A major party is in full swing. The crowd is mindlessly
drunk. One OLD TIMER is struggling to play the piano and he
is doing a rotten job of it. Standing above him on the ancient
upright's top is FELICIA, trying desperately to string a few
simple steps together.*

*Seated in another corner is an absolutely plastered MITZI,
surrounded by her disorganised range of beauty products.
Two leathery-faced MINERS' WIVES are covered in revolting
creams.*

MITZI: [slurring] Now what could be more soothing than
coming home after a hard day down the mine to the 'Wo-
Man' in us all. Now don't send any money . . .

*On the other side of the room, another mass of people have
gathered around a table. BERNADETTE and SHIRLEY are in the
middle of a drinking contest. About fifteen empty shot glass
are lined up next to at least another dozen full ones. Both
girls are faltering. SHIRLEY raises up a glass, places it to her
lips . . . and downs the contents. The spectators groan in
agony.*

*BERNADETTE raises her glass. Her eyes are bloodshot.
Drawing a breath, she swallows. 'Ooooooh' from the crowd.*

*Thumping her arms to the table, SHIRLEY lifts another glass
which is shaking in her hand. Eventually . . .*

SHIRLEY: [*slurring*] Shit . . . All I can see is female impersonators . . .

> *SHIRLEY's point of view: eight drag queens spinning round and round. Her head falls forward. Smash. The spectators roar. They crowd in around BERNADETTE, slapping her on the back in congratulations. She too, however, is not in good shape. Her No.1 fan, the big FAT MINER who laughed, helps her up.*

FAT MINER: This has got to be a first. Nobody has ever out-drunk Shirl before. Where did you learn to throw 'em back like that?

> *FELICIA pushes through the mob with a totally obliterated MITZI hanging off her shoulder.*

FELICIA: That's our girl Bernadette. I just knew that stumbling around the pub circuit with 'Les Girls' for two hundred years must have taught her something.

> *BERNADETTE is not about to fight back. She is busy trying to hold down her booze.*

FAT MINER: You're a bloody marvel, Bernie!

BERNADETTE: Bernadette, please.

FAT MINER: What was that?

BERNADETTE: [*still struggling*] My name isn't Bernie.

> *FELICIA now has MITZI strung over her shoulder.*

FELICIA: She said her name isn't Bernie . . . [*giggling*] It's Ralph.

> *BERNADETTE is drunk, but hearing the word 'Ralph' sobers her up very quickly. She stares after her stumbling companions with eyes like poison.*

39. INT. BROKEN HILL HOTEL ROOM — NIGHT

The front door flies open, sending FELICIA and the legless MITZI tumbling onto the bed. BERNADETTE is behind.

BERNADETTE: What did you call me?

FELICIA: What did you call me what?

BERNADETTE: [*fighting to remain composed*] What did you call me back there, in the bar?

> *FELICIA is genuinely confused. And suddenly she remembers.*

FELICIA: Sorry. Ralph.

A large seismic explosion goes off inside BERNADETTE's *brain. She loses control and lunges across the bed, taking the unsuspecting* FELICIA *by surprise.*

MITZI *begins to snore. She is totally oblivious to the erupting carnage.* BERNADETTE *has* FELICIA *in a head lock, slamming her head first into the bathroom door.* FELICIA *pushes back hard and they tumble over, pulling the drapes down on top of them. Smash!*

FADE OUT

40. EXT. BROKEN HILL HOTEL — DAY

Bag in hand, TICK *greets the morning sunshine like a vampire. A hangover is evident. Behind him is an infuriated* BERNADETTE *followed by* ADAM. *The verbal war continues. They are screaming at each other.* TICK *is not paying attention.*

CARRYING ON TO . . .

41. EXT. BROKEN HILL HOTEL BALCONY — DAY

Shading his eyes from the glare, TICK *moves ahead of his companions. He stops dead with the sight before him. The others are too busy to notice.* BERNADETTE's *voice eventually trails off when she finally registers the sight before them.*

Splattered right down the side of the bus before them in blood-red paint are the unforgettable words, 'AIDS FUCKERS GO HOME'. Everybody falls silent. The hurt on TICK's *face is immeasurable.*

42. EXT. GAS STATION — DAY

ADAM *is filling 'Priscilla' with fuel. His mood is now quite sombre. He walks inside to pay.*

43. INT. GAS STATION — DAY

Pushing through the rusty old door, ADAM *is confronted by a little OLD MAN. They exchange 'Good mornings'.*

44. INT. BUS — DAY

TICK is stone-faced at the wheel. BERNADETTE sits behind.

TICK: It's funny, you know. No matter how tough I think I'm getting, it still hurts.

45. INT. GAS STATION — DAY

The OLD MAN slides a large box into the waiting hands of ADAM.

OLD MAN: Hope it still works. Don't have much call for it out here. Where you blokes from?
ADAM: Uranus.
> *The OLD MAN has never heard of Uranus, but he smiles and waves goodbye.*

46. EXT. DESERT/MINGARY TURN-OFF — DAY

'Priscilla' is purring along the tar sealed road.

47. INT. — BUS

TICK is still driving. He spots what he has been looking for.

TICK: There.
> *The hydraulic brakes squeal to a halt as the bus pulls up before a wide dirt track snaking endlessly off into the desert. BERNADETTE, lounging down the back with a drink in one hand and a magazine in the other, issues a warning.*
BERNADETTE: I hope you know what you're doing.
TICK: If we stick to the sealed road, we'll be at it for at least another two days.
> *ADAM turns back to BERNADETTE with an enormous*

cheesy grin. BERNADETTE is stone-faced.
BERNADETTE: Take the short cut.
The bus turns onto the track. LOGOWOMAN jogs past.

48. EXT. DUSTY TRACK — DAY

The red desert is flashing past to the accompaniment of some very grand opera. Suddenly, FELICIA appears in full frame, mouthing the Italian soprano in perfect synchronisation.

PULLING OUT . . .

Dressed in a truly massive and spectacular frock, FELICIA is on top of 'Priscilla', sitting in a giant silver shoe. The enormous twelve foot tails on her garment are twirling lyrically in the burning breeze. It is a sight to behold.

49. INT. BUS — DAY

BERNADETTE is driving with a very unhappy look on her face.

BERNADETTE: One more push, I'm going to smack his face so
   hard he'll have to stick a toothbrush up his arse to clean
   his teeth.

50. EXT. DUSTY TRACK — DAY

The scrub is dense and harsh. 'Priscilla' carries her dusty tail like a great yellow veil on a four-wheeled wedding dress. The sun is getting low in the western sky.

INSIDE THE BUS

BERNADETTE is driving, safely out of ear-shot. ADAM, still half clad in the Bus Top costume, is fixing TICK a drink.

TICK: I told you not to use the 'R' word, and what did you go
   and do?
ADAM: I was only having fun.

TICK: Fun? What else do you do for amusement? Slam your fingers in car doors? What's the point?

ADAM: I like seeing people get hot-headed, ok? It gives me a kick.

TICK: Is it true that when you were born the doctor turned around and slapped your mother? What sort of bent childhood did you grow up in, Adam Whitely?

51. INT. ADAM'S BATHROOM. FLASHBACK — DAY

A very cute six-year-old ADAM *sticks his head into the bathroom to face his* UNCLE, *who is lounging luxuriously in the deep end of the bath, toying seductively with the chain leading down between his legs to the bath plug below.*

UNCLE: Adam? Come in here, boy. Come and sit over here.

ADAM obediently walks into the bathroom and closes the door.

[*smiling*] Would you like to have some fun with Uncle Barry? We're going to play a special game, but you can't tell anybody. Never, ever, ever. Now what I want you to do, is put your hand down here and pull very gently, OK? Very gently.

The child looks down into the water and shrugs his shoulders. Suddenly, CLUNK! UNCLE's *eyes open wide and he starts to croak.* ADAM *lifts his hands out of the water holding the plug and chain in one hand.* UNCLE *is draining of colour, unable to scream through the pain.*

Oh, Jesus Christ, Adam! Get help!

The boy just stands there, watching his UNCLE *turn white.*

Adam, Uncle Barry's ping pongs are stuck in the drain. Get mummy!

ADAM: No.

UNCLE: [*in agony*] What do you mean, no?

BACK IN THE BUS

52. INT. BUS — DAY

ADAM: [*struggling to hold back the hysteria*] Never ever ever ever. . .

TICK falls down on the floor of the bus holding his stomach in fits of laughter. He cannot stop. ADAM soon joins him.

You know the best part? Mum was out playing golf and the dirty old fuck was stuck there for seven hours! And I thought they were small and wrinkled before they got in the water!

53. EXT. DUSTY TRACK — NIGHT

'Priscilla's' headlamps are the only light in the pitch black desert.

54. INT. BUS — NIGHT

Halfway down the aisle, TICK is sewing a dress. BERNADETTE has her finger stuck in a jar of 'Wo-Man' facial cleanser and ADAM is steering 'Priscilla' around the dumbstruck rabbits on the road.

ADAM: Hey. I got a joke. Who wants to hear a joke?
    Silence.
    Come on, Bernie. It's so funny, you'll laugh so hard your lashes will curl up by themselves.
BERNADETTE: Do tell us your hilarious joke.
    TICK smiles. This is a step in the right direction.
ADAM: OK. Well, many moons ago there was this famous bunch of Indians called the Fukawie Tribe.
    BERNADETTE rolls her eyes. Every man and his dog has heard this.
    And one day the son of the Great Indian Chief says to his father, Dad, why is my friend Little Hawk called Little Hawk?' And his father says . . .
TICK and BERNADETTE: [*mimicking*] Why do you ask, Two Dogs Fucking?
ADAM: That's not the end of the joke. So anyway, back to me. Shit!
    Clunk! They all lurch forward. The bus is decelerating rapidly.
TICK: What's happening?

ADAM: I don't know.

> ADAM *begins to pound the pedals without success.*
>
> *'Priscilla' chugs slowly to the side of the road and comes to a deafening standstill. Silence.* ADAM *turns over the ignition. Splutter, splutter. Nothing. The Queen of the Desert is as dead as a door nail.*

BERNADETTE: Oh my God . . .

SLOW FADE OUT

55. EXT. DUSTY TRACK — EARLY MORNING

FADE IN

A lizard basks in the morning sun. The bus door hisses open and delivers its sleep encrusted occupants onto the turf. TICK, ADAM *and* BERNADETTE *drop from the stairs one by one and scan the vast horizon. 'Priscilla' rests beside a cleared dirt track — a feeble excuse for a roadway, set deep in the middle of nowhere. She is but a mere spot on the horizon. Nobody wants to say anything, but they are all thinking the same thing.* BERNADETTE *raises a pair of sunglasses to her eyes and sighs.*

BERNADETTE: Oh Felicia . . . Where the Fuk-a-wie?

FELICIA: [*off*] Shit! Shit! Shit!

56. EXT. DUSTY TRACK CAMP — DAY

A delicious breakfast is laid out. The mood is very pensive. TICK *stands under the hood, lavishly smearing 'Wo-Man' cold cream all over the motor to no avail. Moving back to the camp fire, he sits down beside* ADAM *who is spooning out the food.* BERNADETTE *is angry.*

TICK: Well, I've had a look around, and I think we can safely assume that I now know less about motor cars than I did when I first lifted up that . . . bonnety thing.

BERNADETTE: Now what?

TICK: Let's just not think about it for the moment and eat breakfast, shall we?

BERNADETTE: That's a novel idea! Let's stuff ourselves to death! Imagine the headlines . . . 'Whales beach themselves in the outback . . . Mystery Broomsticks Dead in Drag'.

ADAM: There's no point in walking back. The only life I saw for the last million miles were the hypnotised bunnies, and most of them are now wedged in the tyres.

ADAM wanders off to the bus.

TICK: Somebody's sure to drive past. We'll keep the fire burning.

BERNADETTE: Yes, and toast marshmallows and chill champagne for when they arrive. What if they don't drive past?

TICK: Look, you're not helping here. Just eat your hormones.

BERNADETTE: Hell. Why didn't we stick to the main road?

TICK: What difference does it make now?

BERNADETTE: You got us into this, Anthony Belrose, and I suggest you start thinking about how to get us back or I don't fancy your chances of ever trying to be a husband again!

Silence.

Jesus. What are we going to do?

ADAM: We are going to start off with a little face lift.

ADAM approaches the camp with the large box he bought at the last gas station. He holds a paint brush in the air.

Nothing like a new frock to brighten up your day.

57. EXT. DUSTY TRACK CAMP — DAY

Splat! A well dunked paint brush slams against the side of the dusty bus. The colour?

TICK: Purple?

ADAM: It's not purple. It's lavender. What do you think?

TICK: It's nice . . . in a hideous sort of a way.

BERNADETTE jumps from the bus in her best walking shoes and makes her way toward the road.

Where are you going?

BERNADETTE: If you think I'm going to sit around watching Picasso take on the public transport system, you've got another think coming. I'll be back with the cavalry in a couple of hours.

ADAM slaps on more paint as BERNADETTE disappears.

ADAM: There goes a transsexual, last seen heading south. We all called her Bernie, but her real name was . . .

TICK: Adam!

LAP DISSOLVE

58. EXT. DUSTY TRACK CAMP — DAY

The sun overhead is at its hottest. BERNADETTE has been walking for quite some time. She pauses for a drink, and wipes her forehead. Damn! Her make-up is beginning to run.

59. EXT. DUSTY TRACK CAMP — DAY

ADAM is in his overalls on top of the half purple bus. His hair is protected from the slopping paint brush by a hair net.

60. INT. BUS — DAY

TICK is lying down, staring blankly and fanning himself. Across the bus, he spots a full-length lime-green evening gown.

61. EXT. DUSTY TRACK/SOME MORE MILES UP — DAY

The desert is absolutely vast. There is not a sign of life for miles. Nothing but a small wandering ant that we soon recognise as BERNADETTE. She has a long way to go.

62. EXT. DUSTY TRACK CAMP — DAY

ADAM is not far off completion. He pauses for a rest and looks off into the desert. About a hundred yards away is TICK, clad in full frock but no wig. He is rehearsing to himself. Humming a few bars of a song, he takes a step forward, twirls around, and takes a few steps back. Turn, turn, kick, turn . . . not bad.

63. EXT. DUSTY TRACK/SOME MORE MILES ON — DAY

Way ahead in the distance, a little plume of smoke. It's a car, and it's coming this way. BERNADETTE cannot contain herself.

BERNADETTE: Help! Help!

64. INT. CAR — DAY

PA and MA are driving in a leisurely manner across the desert. Suddenly . . .

MA: What's that, Pa?
PA: What?
MA: Up there, you nong. Looks like a woman.
　　　From their vehicle, a figure can be seen up ahead waving its arms. The vehicle begins to slow down as it approaches the desperate figure. Finally at a standstill, MA and PA wind down their window to meet an exhausted woman.
BERNADETTE: Oh, thank God.
　　　MA and PA stare blankly at BERNADETTE, whose face is a complete disaster. Her mascara has run, her foundation is pouring down her neck, her dribbling eye shadow has become a multi-rainbowed mess and her false eyelashes have curled up and died!

65. EXT. DUSTY TRACK CAMP — AFTERNOON

Approaching the camp is MA and PA's four-wheel drive. BERNADETTE is in the back.

BERNADETTE: Thank you. I can't tell you how grateful I am.

ON TOP OF THE BUS

ADAM stops painting on hearing the car engine. TICK looks round from the rock he has been rehearsing on.

INSIDE THE CAR

PA steers into the camp area in front of the bus. BERNADETTE leaps out of the jeep as ADAM runs around.

ADAM: Bernie, I never thought I'd be so glad to see you.
> *MA and PA are suddenly taken by the sight of another man clad in a full-length gown running toward them from around the side of the bus.*

TICK: I was just drawing up the will.
> *TICK and ADAM wrap their arms around BERNADETTE whilst MA and PA watch on helplessly. After all the excitement, BERNADETTE turns back to her saviours.*

BERNADETTE: Tony, Adam, come and meet our saviours. This is Mr and Mrs Spencer.

ADAM AND TICK: Hello.
> *The man in a dress, the boy in the hair net and the woman with the runny make-up are all beaming with delight . . . Then . . . PA slams his foot onto the accelerator. The wheels tear at the dirt, spewing a thick escape cloud into everybody's faces. The vehicle spins back towards the road at high speed. ADAM gives chase.*

ADAM: No! Wait!
> *Too late. The car has gone. TICK and BERNADETTE lower their hands with the settling dust. ADAM turns back and stares at the pathetic sight before him.*

Oh shit. Oh, for goodness sake. Look at yourself, Mitz!
> *TICK suddenly remembers he is in a dress. He looks down in shock.*

How many times have I told you? Green is not your colour!

66. EXT. DUSTY TRACK CAMP — DUSK

Sitting around the fire are a miserable TICK and BERNADETTE.

TICK: Do you think about Trumpet much?

BERNADETTE: No. Trumpet was just a nice kid who had a thing about transsexuals. Lots of people do. Sort of a bent status symbol. You know, 'Did you know my girlfriend used to be a boyfriend?' That sort of thing. Always good for a supper invite. Still, it was better than nothing.

>*ADAM approaches with a guitar under one arm, slipping a cassette into the large ghetto-blaster.*

ADAM: Nothing. Nothing for miles.

>*Music fills the night sky. ADAM begins to sing along to Abba's 'Fernando'. On recognising the tune, BERNADETTE leans over and stops the tape.*

BERNADETTE: I've said it once and I won't say it again . . . No more fucking Abba!

>*TICK gets to his feet.*

TICK: OK, if we have the time, we may as well put it to good use. Come on, girls, off your snatches. Rehearsal time.

67. EXT. DUSTY TRACK CAMP — DUSK

Lit only by the fire, TICK begins to instruct BERNADETTE and ADAM in the routine he had been practising that afternoon. Turn, turn, kick, turn. This is the first time we actually see them perform together, working perfectly in synchronised harmony. As the finale of the piece approaches, they twirl around and see an ABORIGINAL MAN. Everybody screams.

After a moment, calm prevails. The ABORIGINAL MAN looks from one to another. His mouth breaks into a broad smile.

ABORIGINAL MAN: Hello. Nice night for it.

68. EXT. ABORIGINAL CAMP — NIGHT

Three tray-top trucks surround a huge open fire. An ABORIGINAL GROUP are lounging around, listening to a GUITAR PLAYER and SINGER. It is all very relaxed. Suddenly the music stops. Standing sheepishly beside the ABORIGINAL MAN who discovered them, are TICK, ADAM and BERNADETTE. There is a deathly silence.

TICK: I think we just crashed a party.

ABORIGINAL MAN: No. Come on. You'll be right.

The music resumes. The three are escorted to a sofa near the fire.

ABORIGINAL MAN: Here. Welcome to my office.

ADAM: Bernice, I don't know what could have possibly possessed you to wear *that* to a corroboree!

BERNADETTE: Shut your face.

The threesome stare on in silence.. The scenario before them is becoming quite hypnotic. The fire is raging. TICK watches the glowing ashes rise high into the night sky. As he looks up, he sees the ABORIGINAL MAN watching them. He smiles. The GUITAR PLAYER and SINGER finish their song. TICK begins to clap. BERNADETTE and ADAM quickly join in.

TICK: Bravo!

ADAM: Fabulous!

Clap, clap . . . clap . . . They stop. Silence again.

TICK: Well, girls, I guess it's our turn.

69. EXT. ABORIGINAL CAMP — NIGHT

Music blasts from a small tape deck. MITZI comes twirling into frame, all smiles, and begins to mime 'I Will Survive'. BERNADETTE and FELICIA flank her from both sides, and we recognise it as the number they have been rehearsing all afternoon. The audience are all smiling from ear to ear. They think it is hilarious! The girls are really laying it on! BERNADETTE and MITZI fall back as FELICIA begins an elaborate dance solo. Finding a moment . . .

BERNADETTE: Hey. Take a look at that!

MITZI looks over toward the ABORIGINAL MAN who is on his feet, mimicking FELICIA. He is having a whale of a time! An enormous smile spreads across MITZI's face.

MITZI: I've got an idea . . .

QUICK CUT TO . . .

70. EXT. ABORIGINAL CAMP — NIGHT

The ABORIGINAL MAN, now in a beautiful sequinned gown, feather boa and heels, stands before the crowd alongside his

three new companions, doing his best to follow their steps. Everyone is roaring with laughter, clapping him on. He does not know the words, but that doesn't matter. The song reaches a shattering climax. The crowd goes wild. They all applaud and scream for more.

FADE OUT

71. EXT. DEEP DESERT — DAY

It is a windy day deep in the outback. The occasional scurry of dust blows up into the faces of the group of ABORIGINALS making their way across the desert. In the middle of them is TICK, dressed up against the cold in a manner resembling T.E. Lawrence. They are all laughing and joking. The ABORIGINAL MAN walks beside him.

ABORIGINAL MAN: So you actually make money by dressing up like a woman?
TICK: Oh sure. You can make a fine living in a pair of heels. Why, Alan, do you want a job?

72. EXT. DUSTY TRACK CAMP — DAY

A willy-willy (dust swirl) engulfs the now-purple bus.

INSIDE THE BUS

ADAM is in the process of clearing out his wardrobe. The autographed Anna from Abba looks on. BERNADETTE is sitting on one of the beds, painting her nails.

ADAM: Oh, if only this dress could talk. You know, sometimes I wonder where I got my taste from. Definitely not my mother! Oh well, serves me right for letting her buy me all these awful clothes.
    BERNADETTE lifts up a sealed jar containing a small brown ball.
BERNADETTE: What's this?
ADAM: That, my darling, is my most treasured possession in the whole wide world.

BERNADETTE examines the small brown object.

BERNADETTE: But what is it?

ADAM: Well, a few years ago, I went on a pilgrimage backstage after an Abba concert hoping to grab an audience with Her Royal Highness Agnetha. Well, when I saw her dashing into the ladies' loo, naturally I followed her in. And after she'd finished her business, I ducked into the cubicle, only to find she'd left me a little gift, sitting in the toilet bowl.

BERNADETTE: What are you telling me? This is an Abba turd?

BERNADETTE looks at the jar in complete horror. ADAM smiles and pulls a huge orange frock from the rack.

ADAM: I know what we can do with this.

73. EXT. DUSTY TRACK CAMP — DAY

Several hundred yards from the bus in the blustery winds stands BERNADETTE, holding a large ball of twine in one hand.

BERNADETTE: [yelling out] Are you right?

Up in front of her quite some distance away is ADAM, down on his hands and knees, adjusting the orange frock which is sprawled across the ground.

ADAM: Hang on. OK, go!

BERNADETTE begins to walk backwards with the twine in one hand. And, rising out of the desert, the horrible orange frock finds new life as a beautiful orange kite! Wrapped around a sex doll, it rises higher and higher into the sky, its arms spread wide. It is the world's first flying drag queen! It climbs high into the sky, twisting and turning against BERNADETTE's twine. It is a wonderful sight.

74. EXT. DUSTY TRACK/SOME MILES UP — DAY

TICK, sitting in the passenger seat of a rickety old truck, is scanning the desert. Suddenly . . .

TICK: There!

Through the windshield, pitted against the bright blue sky many miles away, is the splendour of the flying Orange Drag Queen!

75. EXT. DUSTY TRACK CAMP — DAY

ADAM's skyward attention falters when he hears the sound of an engine. Without a moment's hesitation, he dashes toward the road. A puzzled BERNADETTE looks after him before realising the urgency. Then she, too, hears the car. Confused, she looks to the kite, and then to the road.

BERNADETTE: Fuck it . . .
> *BERNADETTE drops the twine and the kite is away. It spirals toward the heavens, free to fly its own sky.*

76. EXT. DUSTY TRACK CAMP — DAY

ADAM and BERNADETTE arrive just in time to greet an ancient old tow-truck as it lumbers off the road and pulls up before the steadfast 'Priscilla'. TICK climbs from the vehicle along with a very burly gentleman in his late forties. It is BOB, the mechanic.

BOB: Afternoon. What seems to be the problem?
> *BERNADETTE and ADAM are extremely pleased to see him.*

77. EXT. TOWNSHIP/BOB'S STATION — DAY

BOB's faded gas station and garage rests dead centre of the tiny town. Ten people have gathered to watch BOB fix the bus. TICK and ADAM stand helplessly nearby. BERNADETTE bends down to scratch a STRANGE MAN's dog.

BERNADETTE: What a nice dog. What's his name?
STRANGE MAN: Herpes. If she's good, she'll heel.
> *BERNADETTE jumps back from the dog as BOB emerges from the bus.*
BOB: Things get pretty quiet around here. We're a bit

starved for entertainment.

TICK: Glad we could oblige. How does it look?

BOB: Well, your gas tank's chock-a-block full of crud. Travelling on a rough road on a low tank chucked it all up into the motor. Your fuel line's blocked and your injectors are stuffed.

TICK: So does that mean you can fix it?

BOB: In the short term. What you blokes need is a new gas tank.

TICK: I don't suppose you have one lying around. . .

BOB: [laughing] No. Sorry. I could pick one up in Coober Pedy in about a week. When do you have to be in Alice?

TICK: Six days.

BOB: Well, we can clean it out and hope for the best. It might make it. Won't know unless you give it a try.

Suddenly, a small Filipino woman emerges from one side of the garage carrying a tea-tray. It is CYNTHIA, BOB's feisty wife.

CYNTHIA: Lemonade here I make.

BOB: That's very nice, darling. But please go back inside.

CYNTHIA: [ignoring him] Lemonade, here I make, lemonade for guests.

BOB: No, darling, please.

CYNTHIA suddenly turns on him in some harsh Asian language. BOB falls immediately quiet. CYNTHIA smiles and holds the tray out toward BERNADETTE.

CYNTHIA: [to BOB] Putang ina mo! [son of a bitch!]

She turns toward the others.

I make chocolate crackles.

Piled high on the plate before BERNADETTE is a mass of very quickly melting chocolate crackles.

78. INT. BOB'S HOUSE — NIGHT

The meal is under way. ADAM and TICK are dressed rather casually, BERNADETTE a little more up-market. The food is on the table. CYNTHIA lifts her gift jar of 'Wo-Man' over the meal.

CYNTHIA: Thank you. We put cream on?

TICK: No, no. It's face cream. For face.

BERNADETTE: Bob, Cynthia, thank you. I love lamb with meringue.

BOB: Thank you for the company. Like I said earlier, new faces are rather hard to come by out here. If you don't mind me asking, what are you doing off the highway?

Embarrassed silence. TICK takes a bite of his bread.

ADAM: Now that's a good question.

BOB: Glad you bothered. We don't get your type out here very often.

Silence once more. BOB realises his mistake.

CYNTHIA: Me like to sing. Me like . . .

BOB talks over the top of her.

BOB: Yeah, pretty damn quiet. Thought of opening a video business for a while, but I suppose we've got to wait to get televisions first.

CYNTHIA is trying to break in and change the direction of the conversation.

CYNTHIA: Me perform for you. Me dance too.

BOB: [breaking in] My wife used to be in the entertainment business.

CYNTHIA: Yeah. You perform here?

BOB: Are you thinking of performing here? I mean you've got to be here at least another night.

TICK: The thought hadn't really crossed my mind.

BOB: Well, why not? I could have a word to Wally in the pub. Everybody would love it!

TICK: I don't think our show would go down too well out here.

BOB: If you don't mind me asking, what kind of cabaret do you do?

TICK is just about to answer but ADAM beats him to the punch line.

ADAM: We dress up in women's clothes and parade around mouthing the words to other people's songs.

BOB: You mean, sort of like those . . . what do you call them? 'Les Girls'?

Their eyes all widen like saucers, BERNADETTE's in particular!

Oh yeah, I've seen them. Way back in Sydney when I was a young bloke. Fantastic. Just terrific!

TICK places his hand on BERNADETTE's shoulder.

TICK: Bob, you're looking at probably the most famous 'Les Girls' ever produced.

BOB: You're kidding me.

BERNADETTE: Oh, give me a break. I wasn't that famous.

TICK: I'm not joking.

BOB: What? I wouldn't really have seen you. That must have been thirty years back.

ADAM: Oh, you'd be surprised.

CYNTHIA: Me perform for you. Me sing!

BOB: No. Cynthia. You no perform. They perform. Not you.

> CYNTHIA *begins to get angry. The swearing begins again.*

CYNTHIA: Putang ina mo! Manigas ka! [Son of a bitch! Get Stuffed!]

> BOB *looks at her pleadingly, and she slows to a spoilt pout.*

BOB: A real live 'Les Girls' show? Right! This calls for a celebration.

> *A very excited* BOB *races to the cupboard and retrieves a bottle of sparkling red champagne.* TICK *looks to* BERNADETTE *in silent fear.*

79. INT. PUB — NIGHT

Most of the town's drinking population is in the pub tonight. The word of a performance has spread. The air is thick with the stench of cigarettes and stale beer. A long bar stems the entire length of the room. Behind the bartender himself is a doorway which leads to the stores room. A face is peeking out.

80. INT. STORE ROOM — NIGHT

BERNADETTE looks nervously at the crowd out front. MITZI *is applying the last of the make-up,* FELICIA *is stuffing her bra.*

BERNADETTE: Maybe this isn't such a good idea.

FELICIA: Oh shut your twat. Our frocks were the sensation of Broken Hill, remember?

BERNADETTE: There was a K-Mart in Broken Hill. At least they knew what a frock was. Christ, you should see what this woman's wearing. It's not a frock, it's a piece of corrugated iron!

BERNADETTE quickly pulls her head away as BOB approaches. He knocks politely.

BOB: Can I come in?

FELICIA: Only if you're single.

BOB enters and is very impressed with what he sees.

BOB: Oh, you look . . . incredible.

MITZI: Where did we find this guy?

FELICIA: Just keep dishing out the compliments, Bob! Flattery will get you everywhere! Now where's that lovely wife of yours?

BOB: [*touchy*] She's at home. She's not allowed in the pub anymore.

MITZI: Really? Why?

BOB: She's got a problem with alcohol. Every time she gets in the pub, she makes a complete fool of herself.

MITZI nods in understanding.

MITZI: Oh I know how she feels.

BOB: Well, we're all waiting. Are you ready?

BERNADETTE: Bob, we're having second thoughts.

BOB: You can't back out now. Every man and his dog is out there.

BERNADETTE: They're not chained up by any chance . . . ?

BOB: Oh, you blokes . . . sorry . . . you girls. Look, you'll be fine. Take my word for it.

81. INT. BOB'S HOUSE — NIGHT

A very angry CYNTHIA is sitting in the kitchen with her bottom lip stuck out. Her chair is facing a well-out-of-reach cupboard positioned high above the fridge, the handles of which have been padlocked together. Suddenly there is a distant roar of laughter from the pub. There is big fun going on out there.

CYNTHIA: Manga hayop! Manga animal! Papakita kosakanila akoy kakanta at akoy sasa yaw! [Animals! Bunch of animals! I'll show them. I'll sing, I'll dance!]

CYNTHIA takes a broom and climbs atop the chair, jamming the handle under the padlock. She plies it hard and finally, smash!

CYNTHIA falls forward as the cupboard flies open. She lands on the floor with a thud and is suddenly surrounded by bouncing ping-pong balls. She gets to her feet and looks up happily. Inside the cupboard is a mass of alcohol, paint brushes, pipes and ping-pong balls.

82. INT. PUB — NIGHT

The house-lights dim slightly. Music begins to rise above the noise of the crowd. One by one, heads turn toward the bar. Accompanied by a huge fanfare, FELICIA explodes from the store room. She quickly mounts a make-shift staircase which leads to the top of the bar, followed closely by BERNADETTE and MITZI. All eyes are on them. FELICIA spins to her audience and begins to mime.

The girls perform. They swirl endlessly across the bar. The reaction is mixed. Some laugh, some frown. BOB is at the back of the room smiling enthusiastically. The high heels click across the bar. As the finale approaches, the girls fall into positions, raise their arms smiling, and await the applause. The number finishes.

Silence. BOB begins to clap heartily. He then looks around and realises he is on his own. The girls look desperately from side to side. Not a sound. Suddenly . . .

Ooowww! The howl of a she-devil. All attention suddenly turns to the front door of the pub. Standing before them wearing a hat and the tiniest of outfits, is CYNTHIA. BOB's face suddenly drops in horror. Every man in the pub begins to smile.

CYNTHIA makes her way toward the bar, running her hands over her body in a very suggestive manner. The crowd goes wild. They have seen this before.

The drag queens climb quickly from the bar in confusion. The powerless and cowering BOB has not moved.

BERNADETTE: What the hell's going on?
> *CYNTHIA climbs on top of the bar and begins her show. The men all around are losing control. CYNTHIA reaches into her cleavage and brings out three ping-pong balls, before slowly undoing her zipper.*

MITZI: [*horrified*] She's not . . . is she?
> *We cannot see what is happening on the bar, but we*

have a pretty good idea by the reactions on the disbelieving faces. FELICIA is laughing like a schoolboy.

FELICIA: Oh, you can't do that with a ping-pong ball!

BERNADETTE: You want to bet?

And all three faces measure up to the sight before them. The crowd is groaning in an odd mixture of laughter and horror. BOB can't look.

MITZI: [*mortified*] Oh no . . . No . . . Oh God!

Pop! A ping-pong ball flies into the audience. The whole pub begins to scream. Pop! Another ball sails through the air and lands in a glass of beer. Pop! BOB cannot stand it any longer. He pushes through the crowd and tries to drag the deliriously happy CYNTHIA from the bar. The mob begin to 'boo'. The little Filipino woman turns on her bullying husband, and the fight is on.

FADE OUT

83. EXT. BOB'S GARAGE — DAY

FADE IN

The front door of the garage flies open. A seething CYNTHIA emerges, dragging a suitcase toward the car.

BOB: Darling. Don't go. There's nothing we can't work out.

CYNTHIA: You no good man.

BOB: Don't be silly.

CYNTHIA: You want good wife. You be good husband.

BOB: Darling, don't go.

CYNTHIA: I not like you anyway. You got little ding-a-dong.

She climbs into the vehicle and disappears in a cloud of dust. BOB turns around to find TICK, ADAM and BERNADETTE standing around a repacked bus, staring at him. They are still a little stunned. BOB forces a smile.

BOB: Some days, you just shouldn't get out of bed. [*Struggling*] If you want my opinion, I think you should stay here until I get back from Coober Pedy with a new tank. But then again, you listened to my last opinion.

BERNADETTE: Forget it, Bob. It's time we made a move. I'm just a gifted amateur round here. There's no way a nice frock and a catchy tune can compete with three ping-

pong balls, two cigarettes and a pint of beer.

BOB is very embarrassed.

TICK: If we break down, we break down. I'll play it safe and stick to the main drag. Pardon the pun. Well, goodbye Bob. Thanks for a very educational stay.

ADAM: Yes. I'd do anything to be able to open a bottle like that.

Finally TICK and ADAM mount the stairs to the bus. BERNADETTE is last on board. She smiles. BOB takes her hand.

BOB: Bernadette, it has certainly been an honour meeting a member of 'Les Girls'.

BERNADETTE: And may I say it has been an honour to have met a gentleman. Believe me, Bob, these days gentlemen are an endangered species.

BERNADETTE gets inside and stands at the door of the bus.

Unlike bloody drag queens, who just keep breeding like rabbits.

TICK turns over the engine and 'Priscilla' pulls away. BOB raises a smile. Suddenly, splutter! The bus begins to choke. The expression on BOB's face fades with the sound of the motor. It slowly pulls to the side of the dirt track just outside the station. It is still running, but only just. BOB draws a big breath. TICK sticks his head out of the window and smiles.

TICK: Bob, fancy a free ride to Coober Pedy?

84. EXT. END OF DUSTY TRACK — DAY

'Priscilla' thunders across the dirt track back in search of the tar-sealed road.

85. INT. BUS — DAY

BOB is stowing his bag down the back of the bus.

ADAM: Now listen, Bob. Let's get a few things straight. *We* may wear the frocks around here, but that doesn't mean that *you* wear the pants.

BOB: Where do I sleep?

ADAM: Oh, anywhere that takes your fancy.

BOB: [smiling] The roof will do me fine.

> BOB makes his way toward the front of the bus towards BERNADETTE and driver TICK.

TICK: Thank you, Bob. I don't know what to say.

BOB: That's all right. I may as well get there a few days earlier. A bit of R and R. God knows I need it.

MUSIC BEGINS

86. EXT. ROAD TO COOBER PEDY — DAY

MUSIC CARRIES OVER

The return of high Italian opera. FELICIA is on the roof again, another spectacular frock trailing out behind her. She is a rainbow of colour and beauty.

INSIDE THE BUS

87. INT. BUS — DAY

BOB is behind the wheel with BERNADETTE seated beside him.

BOB: May I ask you a personal question? I mean, if you don't mind.

BERNADETTE: Sure.

BOB: [struggling] Why? Why do you . . . you know . . .

BERNADETTE: You mean the sixty-four thousand dollar question ...

88. INT. CHILDHOOD LOUNGE ROOM. FLASHBACK. DAY.

The small late 1950s suburban lounge room is filled with Christmas decorations. Crowded into the corner around the tree are BERNADETTE's MUM, DAD and little SISTER. Sitting quietly to one side is a tiny eight-year-old BOY (BERNADETTE). They are all in the middle of unwrapping presents. In contrast to the BOY, the little SISTER is gently tearing the paper from her large box as her MUM talks her through it.

MUM: That's the girl. Now don't tear the wrapping paper. Just slide the ribbon off and we can see what Santa's brought you! Here it comes now. What is it? It's a . . . it's a [*confused*] . . . cement mixer.

> *The equally confused* SISTER *is now holding an unwrapped cement mixer in her hands.* MUM *draws a deep breath and turns to the smiling* BOY, *who is already surrounded with unwrapped dolls, tea sets and horse figurines.* MUM *is not happy.*

Have you been changing the cards around again, Ralph?

BACK IN THE BUS

89. INT. BUS -- DAY

BERNADETTE is staring out at the open road with a broad smile.

BERNADETTE: So I guess I had no choice in the matter.

> *Suddenly the bus lurches forward. 'Priscilla' is beginning to buck. There is an almighty crash on the roof followed by . . .*

FELICIA: [*off, furiously*] Oh, for fuck's sake! Watch where you're driving, you stupid bitch! What are you trying to do, fucking kill me or something?

BOB: My fault.

FELICIA: [*nicely again*] Sorry Bob. I thought it was Bernadette.

> *The bus begins to choke and splutter.* BOB *raises his eyebrows in concern.*

90. EXT ROAD TO COOBER PEDY/CAMP — NIGHT

BOB is under the bonnet working on the motor. BERNADETTE is alongside holding the torch. A waltz is playing on the tape deck. Off to one side, TICK is teaching ADAM how to waltz. They twirl around the fire giggling like children. BOB is watching from the corner of his eye.

ADAM: Who taught you to waltz?

TICK: My wife.

ADAM: Oh, how sweet, you and the Mrs. down at Arthur Murray's every Tuesday night practising your little hearts out. Makes me want to sick up.

BOB is genuinely surprised by the news.

BOB: Married?

BERNADETTE: Yes, married. We have only recently discovered that young Anthony here 'bats for both teams'.

TICK: [*embarrassed*] I do not.

ADAM: Oh, so we're straight.

TICK: No.

ADAM: We aren't? So we're a doughnut puncher after all.

TICK: No.

ADAM: Then what the hell are we?

TICK: [*laughing*] I don't fucking know!

Suddenly, a small light emerges from the darkness behind.

BERNADETTE: What the fuck's that?

Everybody turns in fear. Out of the darkness comes a jogging LOGOWOMAN. She is rugged up against the cold with a helmet and light attached to her head. Trailing along behind is a buggy, connected to her waist. She runs with purpose right past the stranded bus without stopping. ADAM finally speaks.

ADAM: Good evening. Nice night for it. Oh, OK. Goodnight then.

She runs across the firelight and out into the darkness. Everybody is a little stunned.

BERNADETTE: [*off*] What a rude woman!

DISSOLVE TO . . .

91. EXT. ROAD TO COOBER PEDY — MORNING

BOB is under the bonnet of the bus absolutely covered in oil, explaining the mechanics to BERNADETTE, who sits attentively alongside, trying to look interested.

BOB: And that's the power steering pump, and that's the radiator fan.

BERNADETTE: How interesting.

TICK is in the distance, a pile of handbags by his side. He picks one up, twirls it above his head sling shot

*style, and hurls it toward a stacked pile of 'Wo-Man'
cold cream jars. Smash.* ADAM *emerges from behind a
hill.*

ADAM: Hey! Who wants first bath?

MUSIC BEGINS

92. EXT. WATERHOLE — DAY

ADAM leads BERNADETTE, BOB *and* TICK *over the hill to the foot
of a huge lake. Everybody gets excited at the sight of water.*
*ADAM begins to rip off his shirt and hits the drink half
clothed. The others follow.* BERNADETTE *pauses for a moment,
then takes the plunge. There is much hooting and splashing.
A courtly* BOB *helps* BERNADETTE *out of the water.*

BOB: Can I help you, Madam?

MUSIC MERGES INTO SONG

93. EXT. ROAD TO COOBER PEDY — DAY

BOB sticks his head out from under the hood.

BOB: OK. Turn her over.
    TICK *turns the ignition over. 'Priscilla' chokes up for a
    second and finally rumbles to life. Everybody cheers.*
    BOB *drops the hood and clambers aboard. 'Priscilla'
    pulls back out onto the road. Suddenly, splutter!*
    TICK *turns her over again, this time with success.*

94. INT. BUS — DAY

SONG CARRIES OVER

The song is 'I don't care if the sun don't shine'. ADAM *walks
flamboyantly up and down the bus, mouthing the words. He
throws a hand to* TICK, *who takes over the chorus.* BERNA-
DETTE, *sewing, throws in the odd line.*

95. EXT. COOBER PEDY TOWNSHIP — DAY

'Priscilla' cruises slowly down the main street of the mining town. It is a ghostly place, mostly underground.

96. INT. BUS — DAY

BOB is pointing the way.

BOB: That's it over there. It's an OK room with a shower.

TICK and BERNADETTE: Bags first!

ADAM: Is hot water all you can think about?

BERNADETTE: No. A shower, a comfortable bed and a nice meal will do me fine.

ADAM: If you think I'm going to crawl into the sack and watch television you've got another think coming.

BOB: Now look you blokes, watch your back. This is a pretty tough little town. They get up in the morning, they go down a hole, they blow things up and then they come up again. That just about sums it up.

ADAM: Oh fabulous.

BERNADETTE: You're welcome to hang out with us, Bob, if you got nothing better to do.

BOB: I'm meeting some of the boys down at the old drive-in for a booze-up like the old days.

ADAM: I want to go with Bob! I want to go to the boys' club!

BERNADETTE: You'll come and have supper with us, Adam Whitely, or you'll stay in your room by yourself and watch TV.

97. INT. COOBER PEDY UNDERGROUND MOTEL ROOM — NIGHT

A very bored ADAM sits on the end of the bed swinging his legs backward and forward. He then stares blankly at the TV. He moves over to his bag and throws open the top. Flicking mindlessly through a few frocks, he suddenly pauses when he finds a handbag. A smile creeps over his face. ADAM opens the bag and releases a hidden zip. Squeezing his fingers inside, he withdraws a small plastic

bag filled with a fine white powder.

98. INT. COOBER PEDY RESTAURANT — NIGHT

BERNADETTE and TICK are seated in the front window of a quaint little restaurant which overlooks the dusty main street. A bottle of wine sits in the ice bucket. Very civilised.

TICK: He's a good man, our Bob.

BERNADETTE: Yeah. Not my type though.

TICK: Oh, don't come the raw prawn with me. I can spot the fluttering of a beaded lash from three hundred paces.

BERNADETTE: Get out. He's far too old. Mind you, so am I. Did you catch that mail order bride? Why did he marry her? I'm dying to ask.

> *The playful expression on TICK's face immediately changes for the worse.*

BERNADETTE: Oops. Sorry. Don't worry about it. You're the world's best husband, and given the chance, you'd probably be a perfectly good father too.

TICK: Do you really think so?

BERNADETTE: Why? Are you thinking about children?

TICK: Yes, as a matter of fact.

99. EXT. MAIN STREET COOBER PEDY — NIGHT

It is late and the street is mostly deserted. A sleeping dog on a shop front lifts its head to the sound of a most peculiar clicking. A pair of high heel shoes are making their way down the footpath towards the flashing lights of a large video store.

100. INT. VIDEO STORE — NIGHT

The young ATTENDANT looks up casually from his pollywaffle and nearly drops dead with the sight before him. It is, of course, a very overdressed FELICIA. She walks slowly forward, looking around rather dramatically, sniffling the last of the cocaine up her nasal passage. She stops at the cashier's desk and stares at the bewildered boy.

FELICIA: Do you have 'The Texas Chainsaw Mascara'?

101. INT. RESTAURANT — NIGHT

The conversation has turned a little serious.

TICK: Ever wanted kids?
BERNADETTE: Sure. But I've learned not to think about it.
TICK: Do you think an old queen's capable of raising a child?
BERNADETTE: Well, Elizabeth did a pretty good job. Prince Charles is a wonderful boy.
TICK: Edward's still a bit of a worry. And what happens if they turn out like Adam?
BERNADETTE: You stuff them back in and ask for a refund. Stupid little shit. I dread to think what he's up to.

102. EXT. COOBER PEDY DRIVE-IN — NIGHT

Gathered at the base of the crumbling old screen are several raucous miners surrounding an old 16mm projector and a roasting kangaroo. The attention shifts to the lone drag queen who makes her way into the centre of the mob. FELICIA has arrived.

FELICIA: Hello. I'm new in town.
KEGMAN: No kidding.
> *Across the other side of the fire, drinking with a handful of mates, is BOB. On seeing FELICIA, his head drops in horror.*
FELICIA: Could I have a Bloody Mary please?
KEGMAN: It's a beer or nothing, sweetheart.
FELICIA: Well, I'd better have a beer then.
> *FELICIA turns to face the highly amused onlookers.*
> What are you all looking at?
> *FRANK, a rather large and good-looking man, turns to her.*
FRANK: I'm sorry. Didn't mean to stare. We don't usually get women down here.

FELICIA: Oh, so what do women do around here besides watching videos?

FELICIA finally spots the cowering BOB.

Well, well, well. Look who we have here!

FRANK follows FELICIA's glance over to BOB. His eyes are on his beer. He does not look up.

FRANK: You know that bloke, do you?

FELICIA waits for BOB's response, which does not come.

FELICIA: [bitterly] No. So. Who's going to show me the sights?

FRANK is on guard. He raises his drink in a toast.

FRANK: It would be my pleasure.

They raise their beers side by side. FRANK is looking at FELICIA's hand. There is hair on her knuckles. Suddenly he jumps, slapping the beer out of her grasp, sending it crashing to the ground. Then . . .

FELICIA: Well, I suppose a fuck's now out of the question.

FELICIA grabs a beer resting on the bar and throws it into FRANK's face. Then she is off, disappearing into the night. FRANK, still in shock, finally gets a grip on himself. He races out, hot on the heels of FELICIA. Several mates give chase. BOB deliberates for a few moments before downing his beer and running after them.

[*screaming behind as she runs*] Come on boys! Who wants to see my map of Tasmania?

103. INT. COOBER PEDY RESTAURANT — NIGHT

BERNADETTE and TICK are sitting by the picture window, now having finished their meal.

BERNADETTE: So I never had a chance to tell my parents what a wonderful childhood I'd had. They never spoke to me again after I'd had . . . the chop.

TICK takes her hand.

TICK: I have something to tell you.

Behind them, far across the other side of the road, is a drag queen in full flight. BERNADETTE finally catches sight.

BERNADETTE: Oh shit.

104. EXT. MAIN STREET/CAR YARD — NIGHT

FELICIA, still in fits of giggles, rounds the corner of a car yard, running straight to the darkened end before discovering that it is blocked off. She spins around just as FRANK and friends arrive. Her adrenalin is pumping. She smiles.

FELICIA: OK Fellas. Let's not forget how to treat a lady.

FRANK: [*screaming*] You fucking freak!

He throws a bone crunching left hook that connects perfectly with her right jaw. FELICIA falls. This time the shock is hers. FRANK comes at her again, FELICIA lifting her hand in pathetic defence.

FELICIA: No, please . . .

FRANK: Hold him down. Spread his legs.

Two laughing companions move forward, grabbing FELICIA by the legs and spreading them wide. One of the men pulls the dress up to crutch height. FELICIA is sobbing. FRANK takes a few steps back for distance, steadies his boot and runs forward and . . .

BOB: [*screaming*] Frank! Stop!

FRANK falters and stops. BOB is running towards him.

BOB: What the fuck do you think you're doing?

BOB kneels beside FELICIA and pushes the thugs away.

FRANK: You mean you know this cocksucker?

BOB: Get off him, you mongrel! He was joking, OK? Now you leave the bugger alone.

FRANK is in shock. He looks from one to another. Then . . .

FRANK: Get out of there, Bob.

BOB: Cut it out, Frank.

FRANK: Get the fuck out of the way, Bob, or you'll be next.

BOB: Frank . . .

FRANK: [*screaming*] Get out of there!

Suddenly from behind . . .

BERNADETTE: Oh, stop flexing your muscles, you big fucking pile of budgie turd! I'm sure your mates would be much more impressed if you just went back to the pub and fucked a couple of pigs on the bar.

FRANK's eyes widen with horror. He turns to see BERNADETTE and TICK walking briskly toward him. BOB rolls his eyes.

BOB: Bernadette, please.

FRANK: Bernadette? Well I'll be darned! The whole bloody circus is in town! I suppose you want a fuck too!

BERNADETTE is moving straight toward him with eyes of fire.

Come on, Bernadette. Come on and fuck me. That's it.

He spreads his legs wide and starts rubbing his crotch.

Come on, come on and fuck me. Come on. Fuck me.

With all the precision of a well-oiled clock, BERNADETTE swiftly slams a perfect right heel dead centre of FRANK's testicles. He gasps, dropping straight to the ground, groping his crotch. BERNADETTE walks away from the groaning miner victoriously.

BERNADETTE: There. Now you're fucked.

105. INT. HOTEL ROOM — NIGHT

TICK is leaving the room, furious.

TICK: [off] You stupid bloody idiot. Drugs, for Christ's sake! Well, three cheers for you. I hope you're bloody well happy now. Stupid bloody fuckwit!

ADAM begins to cry. BERNADETTE moves quietly beside him on the bed. Eventually . . .

BERNADETTE: It's funny. We all sit around mindlessly slagging off that vile stick-hole of a city. But in its strange way it looks after us. I don't know if that ugly wall of suburbia has been put up to stop them getting in, or us getting out.

ADAM is openly crying now. BERNADETTE cradles him.

Come on. Don't let it drag you down. Let it toughen you up. I can only fight because I've learnt to. Being a man one day and a woman the next is not an easy thing to do.

We see a portrait of the Queen.

106. EXT. COOBER PEDY WRECKER'S — DAY

BOB is talking to a man outside the wrecker's office, which is surrounded by huge old trucks and enormous earth movers. He gets back on board the bus and climbs behind the wheel.

107. INT. BUS — DAY

TICK: Well? Are we bunny hopping all the way to Alice?

BOB: No good. But he says the man to help us is a fair way out of town.

BERNADETTE: Like how fair?

BOB: A couple of hundred clicks fair. No matter. I haven't got anything else to do today. [*Starting the bus*] Let's get out of here. Come on Adam.

> *The bus pulls out onto the road. Looking out the back window, bound up with bandages and looking a bit like a bunny rabbit, is ADAM.*

108. INT. BUS — DAY

BOB is driving, as BERNADETTE studies the map. TICK makes his way down to the back of the bus, where ADAM is still staring silently out of the back window. He makes himself comfortable.

TICK: Some things are said in the heat of the moment. I'm sorry I got angry at you last night, although I dare say you deserved it.

> *The bandages are wrapped around ADAM's very painful-looking jaw.*

Anyway, that's enough of that.

> *ADAM looks at him thankfully.*

You know this is quite an experience sitting here with you now. I can quite safely say that I think your taste in clothing is absolutely terrible. Because you can't say a word, can you? [*Smiling*] This is great fun!

> *ADAM can only react in silent expectation. Suddenly, the bus does a little stall, but the fuel line luckily clears itself. BERNADETTE is surveying the road with a suspicious look on her face.*

BERNADETTE: We're going to have a problem finding this guy with the tank, aren't we?

BOB: Why do you say that?

BERNADETTE: Because he's not out here.

BOB: Oh, he's out here. He's in Alice. Well, I can't go back to

Coober Pedy for a while. Not the most popular bloke in the world back there any more . . .

109. EXT ROAD FROM COOBER PEDY — DAY

'Priscilla' drives off into the desert.

FADE OUT

110. INT. MANILA HOTEL ROOM. FLASHBACK — DAY

A very tacky hotel room. An extremely hungover BOB wakes up in a state of extreme disorientation. He looks hopelessly around for something familiar. It is only now that he sees the small strong Filipino woman sitting in the bed next to him. It is CYNTHIA. She does not smile.

BOB: Hello.
CYNTHIA: Hello.
BOB: Who are you?
CYNTHIA: I your wife.
BOB: Best I be going home then.
      As he pushes himself up, CYNTHIA suddenly turns.
CYNTHIA: [angrily] No, you not going. I coming too. I your wife. See, I your wife.
      She holds a piece of paper to his face. It is a marriage certificate.

111. Ext. ROAD TO ALICE/CAMP — NIGHT

BOB is looking into the fire wistfully, cutting himself another piece of cake.

BOB: Silly girl. Should have done her homework better. She thought I was from Sydney.
TICK: Why in God's name did you bring her home?
      BOB shrugs his shoulders and smiles.
BOB: She was my wife.
ADAM: [muffled] Couldn't you sell her off?
BERNADETTE: Oh, the party is over, everybody. It talks. You

can't keep a good bitch down.

The near empty vodka bottle does the rounds.

TICK: What time do you think we'll get to Alice Springs?

BOB: Late tomorrow arvo?

TICK: And how long do you think you'll be staying?

BOB: I don't know. A couple of days maybe. Hey, a big day for you tomorrow! We all get to meet the Mrs.

ADAM manages to conjure up a smile.

TICK: I saw that smile, Felicia. One word, one derogatory word, and I'm taking you back to your mate in Coober Pedy.

Everybody snickers. TICK gets serious.

Look, please everyone. Tomorrow's going to be a little tough. Please don't make any harder than it has to be.

BERNADETTE: We're only teasing. We won't open our mouths until you give the word. Then it's open season.

More laughter. Then silence. TICK looks up to find BERNADETTE making suggestive faces at him. What? She motions him and ADAM toward the bus. Oh, I get it!

TICK: Oh well, time for bed. Got to look good for the wife in the morning. Come along, Adam! Time for your beauty sleep. Come on.

ADAM is very reluctantly dragged to his feet.

Will you two be joining us?

BERNADETTE: I just thought I'd have one for the road. How about you Bob?

BOB: Sounds good to me.

TICK: All right then. See you in the morning. Night!

TICK and ADAM clamber onto the bus, leaving BERNADETTE and BOB alone.

112. INT. BUS — NIGHT

Once inside, TICK races to the side window and begins to spy. ADAM finally catches on and takes a position beside him.

113. EXT. ROAD TO ALICE/CAMP — NIGHT

The fireside talk is getting personal.

BERNADETTE: Another piece of cake, Bob?

BOB: Ah, no.

BERNADETTE: So, tell me about you.

BOB: Can't complain. Life's a lot simpler now. I spent thirty
years wandering around the world only to find I'm better
off where I started. Not much, but it's my turf.

> Clonk! From behind in the bus, ADAM has fallen off the
> bunk giggling. TICK quickly drops out of view, also
> laughing.

FADE OUT

114. INT. BUS — DAY

*The early morning sunlight strays into the bus. TICK wakes
up. His eyes suddenly widen. He calls to ADAM.*

ADAM: What?

TICK: Guess who didn't come home last night?

> He points across to the two empty bunks. ADAM wakes
> up immediately. He starts to speak before realising that
> he is still in pain. TICK jumps to his feet to look outside.

115. EXT. BUS/ROAD TO ALICE — DAY

*BOB and BERNADETTE are passed out on the ground, fully
clothed, two empty bottles of vodka and a half eaten cake
under BERNADETTE's head. TICK and ADAM are now standing
over the top of them.*

TICK: [whispering] I've waited all my life for this! Bernice has
left her cake out in the rain!

> BERNADETTE slowly, drunkenly, opens her eyelids.

QUICK CUT TO . . .

116. INT. BUS/ROAD TO ALICE — DAY

*TICK is driving with a huge smile on his face, singing 'Hava
Nagila' at the top of his voice. ADAM sits beside him, banging
two pots and pans together.*

Down the back of the bus sit a very hungover BERNADETTE *and* BOB, *each cradling their head in misery.*

                              MUSIC MONTAGE BEGINS

117. EXT. MONTAGE/ROAD TO ALICE — DAY

The border line between South Australia and the Northern Territory flashes past. The road is long and dry. 'Priscilla' rumbles towards the red centre.

118. EXT. ALICE HOTEL — DUSK

                              MUSIC MONTAGE ENDS

'Priscilla' pulls to a halt before the hotel entrance. The occupants tumble out onto the ground. A parking valet eyes them with caution.

TICK: My fucking back is killing me.
BERNADETTE: I need a crap.
BOB: Do you want me to go in?
TICK: No, I'll go.
DOORMAN: Excuse me, sir, you can't park your bus here. Are you planning on staying at the hotel?
TICK: Oh, sorry. Could you direct me to Marion Barber, please. We're the cabaret act from Sydney.
    The DOORMAN *smiles immediately and opens the door.*
DOORMAN: Oh, right. Yeah, well, just go in through to reception and they'll take you right through.
TICK: Thanks.
    TICK *goes inside. The* DOORMAN *turns back to the valet who is still worried about the bus.*
DOORMAN: It's all right, Lenny. These are the drag queens!
    BOB *stops dead in his tracks and looks toward the various startled onlookers.* BERNADETTE *is equally caught out by the comment. Then . . .*
ADAM: [*muffled*] Come on, Bob. Let's go try on your nice new frock.
DOORMAN: [*as they all walk in*] G'day.

119. INT. FOYER/CASINO PART OF HOTEL — DUSK

*TICK walks past the gambling machines towards MARION, who
is on the phone at the bar. She has not noticed him.*

MARION: [*to the phone*] No, those three kegs didn't arrive. I
need them today. Not tomorrow, but today. You're a doll.
[*She hangs up.*] what an arsehole.
    *Suddenly she sees TICK, screams with delight and runs
to him.*
My God. Husband, husband! It's so good to see you!
TICK: Hi 'ya, wife.
    They twirl around. It's a husband and wife thing.
MARION: You're a day late. I was just gathering the search
party. Where are the others?
TICK: Oh, they're outside.
    *MARION looks at her husband. She has a wonderful
face.*
MARION: You've lost weight, you rotten old queer.
TICK: Well, it's about fucking time. I can finally get into that
old one-piece of yours. You know, the one with the
sunflowers.
MARION: You still got that? What the hell do you do with it?
TICK: 'The Poseidon Adventure' routine. You know, Shelley
Winters.
    *They launch into a ridiculous routine together. When it
is over . . .*
Where is he?

120. INT. HOTEL DINING ROOM — DUSK

*MARION leads TICK through to where a MAID is scolding a
small eight-year-old boy, who is responding with
amusement. He looks up. MARION is beaming with joy.*

MARION: Benj, do you remember Tick?
    Silence from both of them. Eventually . . .
BENJAMIN: Hello, Tick.
    TICK cannot take his eyes off his child.
TICK: [*very softly*] Hello.

121. EXT. HOTEL WALKWAY — DUSK

A hotel employee is leading a very vocal BERNADETTE, ADAM and BOB towards the dining room.

QUICK INTERCUT WITH . . .

122. INT. HOSPITAL CORRIDOR FLASHBACK — DAY

Point of view of the DOCTOR and NURSE as seen in the very first flashback — round the corner to the big white doors which are swung open to reveal MITZI (TICK) in full drag. This time the horrified DOCTOR has BERNADETTE, ADAM and BOB, all dressed in nursing uniform, standing behind him.

DOCTOR: Mr Belrose?
MITZI : Yes?
DOCTOR: Congratulations. It's a boy.
　　　As the bucket drops, so does BERNADETTE. She flutters up her lashes and faints . . .

BACK IN THE HOTEL

123. INT. DINING ROOM ENTRANCE — DUSK

. . . hitting her head on the floor as she falls flat out. Everybody races to her aid.

124. INT. ALICE DRESSING ROOMS — NIGHT

A furious BERNADETTE is applying make-up to the bump on her head in the night club dressing rooms. MITZI and FELICIA are all but frocked behind her.

BERNADETTE: For Christ's sake, Mitzi, why didn't you tell us? Why the hell did you have to shock me like that? [*In a pained tone*] This lump is getting bigger by the second. I'm about to make my Northern Territory debut looking like a fucking Warner Brothers cartoon character has hit me over the head with an iron.
FELICIA: I think you look more like a Disney witch myself.

BERNADETTE: Oh, shut your face, Felicia! At least I don't look like somebody has tried to open a can of beans with my make-up!

MITZI is smiling away, applying the last of her face.

MITZI: I'm sorry, girls, I couldn't stand the thought of you two bagging me in a bus for two weeks. Anyway, what difference does it make now?

BERNADETTE About two inches difference to my head for one.

MITZI: Did you get a look at him? He's got my profile, that's for sure.

FELICIA: I think I'm going to be sick.

BERNADETTE gets a little serious.

BERNADETTE: I hate to be practical here, but does he know who you are? I mean, does he know what you do for a living?

MITZI: [*getting defensive*] Well, he knows he has a father in the showbusiness cosmetics industry.

BERNADETTE: Oh Lord, I don't understand!

MITZI: No, you don't understand. So stop trying to. It will be fine.

BERNADETTE calms down and returns to her lump, in the mirror.

BERNADETTE: It had better be.

The dressing room door swings open. MARION comes barging in merrily.

MARION: Stop wearing out that mirror!

FELICIA: You always knock before you enter?

MARION: Always! [*Grabbing stuffing from FELICIA's breasts*] Why? You haven't got anything to hide in there, have you?

MARION lets out her familiar hoot of laughter. MITZI smiles.

All right, girls. You're on in ten minutes.

FELICIA: [*under her breath*] Sweetheart, you've been on ever since you were born.

MARION: Hope you're ready to slay them. The word's out. We've got a big crowd.

BERNADETTE: Like how big?

MARION: A full house.

MITZI: Where's Benj?

MARION: Safe and sound. Asleep in bed. Don't you worry about a thing. OK my little powder puff?

There is a knock at the door.

BOB: [*off*] Can I come in?

BERNADETTE: Now there's a gentleman.

[*calling*] Of course you can, Bob!

BOB enters with a big bunch of flowers.

BOB: My Aunt Minnie in here? Don't mean to barge in. Just want to wish you all good luck.

FELICIA: Thanks Bob.

Shyly BOB gives a bouquet of flowers to BERNADETTE.

BOB: To make up for what happened last time.

BERNADETTE: Thank you. That's so thoughtful.

MARION: All right, girls! Let's get this show on the road. You, out. That's a ten minute curtain call. Good luck.

MARION drags BOB out of the dressing room as the girls scurry for last minute touch ups.

FELICIA: That's quite a wife you got there, Mitzi! What does she do in her spare time? Sand back the hulls of oil tankers with her tongue?

MITZI: She sure is something.

And they are all finally ready. MITZI is so happy, she throws her arms around both BERNADETTE and FELICIA in uncontrolled joy, squeezing them all before . . .

MITZI: Chookers, girls!

FELICIA: Watch my jaw.

BERNADETTE: Be careful of my head.

TICK: Aren't we fabulous?

125. INT. ALICE HOTEL NIGHT CLUB — NIGHT

Two spotlights move randomly across the spangled curtain upon a very upmarket cabaret stage. A strong male voice crackles from the speakers as the opening bars of CeCe Peniston's 'Finally' are heard.

VOICE OVER: Ladies and gentlemen. Lasseter's Casino in Alice Springs presents . . . Miss Mitzi Del Bra, Miss Felicia Jollygoodfellow and Miss Bernadette Bassinger . . . The Sisters of the Simpson Desert!

The curtain opens to reveal the three ladies in the most spectacular outfits yet seen, as Australian flowers. The audience is just visible beneath the heavy follow spots.

Next, they are emus, then frill-necked lizards. Thirdly, and triumphantly, they come down a series of steps in Marie Antoinette outfits which, when re-arranged, become the Sydney Opera House. As the music winds up, they pull back and MITZI *leads the way into a spectacular finale.*

INTERCUT WITH . . .

MITZI *looks triumphantly to* BERNADETTE, *who is also gazing into the crowd. Her face, however, is desperately trying to hold back the disappointment.* MITZI *is confused. She turns to* FELICIA, *whose expression amounts to near devastation. They look at the crowd.*

Before them is a room full of tourists, all seated around serviced tables. The applause is mild, bordering just above the polite, and dying quickly. In the corner is one small group who are clapping madly. It is the ever faithful BOB, *the overjoyed* MARION *and, beside her, a small boy.* MITZI *readjusts her eyes as fear begins to rise up in her throat.*

A smiling BENJAMIN *is clapping cheerfully, looking directly into the eyes of his father, standing centre stage in full drag.* MITZI'S *eyes roll over beneath the burning follow spot and she faints into the front row tables.*

126. INT. DRESSING ROOMS — NIGHT

TICK *is coming back to the land of the living. He is propped up in a chair, surrounded by* MARION, BERNADETTE, BOB *and* ADAM. *They are patting his hand and examining the large scratch on his head.*

ADAM: Come on. Snap out of it.
BOB: Come on, mate.
ADAM: You'll be fine. Come on love.
BOB: That's it mate. You scared us all for a minute.
   Everybody is cluttering around, trying to be helpful, the humour seeping back into the situation.
ADAM: You just had to have that extra little bit of attention,

didn't you? Nice one, lovey. Nice one.

TICK rolls his eyes and looks forward. His expression freezes. BENJAMIN is watching the events with great amusement. TICK forces a smile.

127. INT. ALICE RESTAURANT — NIGHT

It is quite late in the evening. MARION is facing a bandaged and very distressed TICK, who is staring at a daiquiri overflowing with fruit and paper umbrellas.

TICK: Oh shit, what are you doing, Marion?

MARION: Oh shush, drink your Daiquiri.

TICK: I hate bloody Daiquiri.

MARION: No, you don't! You love bloody Daiquiri. Least now I know why drag queens drink from such big glasses. To make their hands look smaller!

MARION hoots with laughter.

TICK: Oh, ha ha ha. What am I meant to say to the boy? I've never been so embarrassed.

MARION: I think you're over-reacting.

TICK: Really?

MARION: Yes. You're just being a drama queen. You're going to have to drop all that shit if you're going to be a good father.

TICK falls very silent.

Don't pretend to be surprised. I've kept my end of the bargain. Now it's your turn. Not forever, maybe just for a couple of months.

TICK: Why now?

MITZI: Because I haven't had a holiday in eight years. I need a rest, Tick, I need some space . . .

After a second, TICK smiles.

TICK: Reminds me of something I said not so long ago.

MARION: Well, I do. And besides, it's time he knew what his father was, anyway.

TICK: That's the problem. I mean, I don't know what to tell him. What do you assume I do? Lie?

MITZI: Assumption, my dear Mitzi, is the mother of all fuck ups. Don't bitch to me, bitch to him.

TICK: Thanks for the free advice.

128. INT. ALICE HOTEL CORRIDOR — NIGHT

BOB is walking down the corridor with the big bunch of flowers in his hand. He stops outside a door and stalls. Then, he cautiously knocks.

BERNADETTE: [*off*] Who is it?
BOB: It's me, Bob.
 After a moment, the door opens. BERNADETTE is getting ready for bed.
Your flowers were being mangled. I thought I'd rescue them for you.
BERNADETTE: Good idea. Thanks.
 She unloads the flowers from his arms. Then silence. There is a moment of deliberation. BOB looks deep into her eyes.

129. INT. ALICE HOTEL ROOM — NIGHT

Playing with his toys on the floor of his room is BENJAMIN. ADAM is watching him sullenly.

BENJAMIN: What's the matter?
ADAM: Nothing.
 BENJAMIN shrugs and continues playing. ADAM is not enjoying the company. He tries a bitchy approach.
ADAM: Do you know what your father does for a living?
BENJAMIN: Yeah.
ADAM: So I suppose you know he doesn't really like girls.
 BENJAMIN thinks about this for a moment.
BENJAMIN: Does he have a boyfriend at the moment?
 The tables turn. The shock is now ADAM's.
ADAM: No.
BENJAMIN: Neither does Mum. She used to have a girlfriend, but she got over her.
 ADAM is now completely stunned. He watches BENJAMIN rise to his feet and walk towards the door. Then . . .
BENJAMIN: Do you want to come and play in my room? I've got Lego.
 ADAM does not know what to say. Finally . . .

ADAM: Sure.

> *A rather dazed* ADAM *gets up and leaves the room with* BENJAMIN.

                                        FADE OUT

130. EXT. ALICE HOTEL — DAY

BOB and ADAM *are waiting beside 'Priscilla' as* BERNADETTE *emerges from the hotel.* TICK *is a little slow this morning.*

BERNADETTE: Come on, Butch. Get a move on. We can't brand the cattle all by ourselves.

> *The* DOORMAN *sweeps open the door to reveal a* TICK *that we have never seen before. Moleskin trousers, western shirt and RM Williams boots. Very masculine and very uncomfortable.*

DOORMAN: Great show last night. Do you always end a number like that?

TICK: Always.

BERNADETTE: How would you like to pick her up every night, Sundance?

DOORMAN: Be a pleasure.

> MARION *arrives from around a corner with a huge picnic basket in one hand and* BENJAMIN *in the other. Talking back to the* DOORMAN.

MARION: I think that might include taking the lady home every evening and tucking her into bed, Jeff.

DOORMAN: What's the pay like, Marion?

> MARION *arrives at the steps of the bus and turns to* TICK.

MARION: Oh, that one's going to get himself into trouble one day, and if you play your cards right, you might just be the lucky fellow.

> TICK *is looking at* BENJAMIN, *obviously embarrassed by the innuendo. He looks up angrily to* MARION, *who is smiling.*

BOB: Come on. All aboard.

> *Everybody climbs aboard and 'Priscilla' pulls away.*

131. EXT. ROAD TO KINGS CANYON — DAY

Leaving the hotel far behind, 'Priscilla' steers her way across

the desert towards the horizon.

132. INT. BUS — DAY

The bus has divided into groups. BERNADETTE *is turning over the road map whilst* BOB *drives. At the back of the bus,* ADAM *is pulling out frocks much to the amusement of* BENJAMIN. MARION *and* TICK *are seated on the central bunks watching their son silently. The atmosphere is not pleasant.*

TICK: Just watch it with the innuendos, Marion. At least give me a clear shot at this.

MARION: You call dressing up as a Xanadu production number a clear shot? Come on Tick. Who's kidding who around here? He sure as shit isn't.

    BENJAMIN is very relaxed, laughing heartily at ADAM.

133. EXT. KINGS CANYON — DAY

The great ancient rocks loom high overhead. Red, warm and ever changing. Dwarfed by their shadow is 'Priscilla', parked in a picnic area, a large blanket spread out on her side. Everyone is playing Charades. ADAM *is performing a 'movie star'. Everybody but* TICK *is screaming and yelling.* ADAM *points to the rock behind and then a river before* MARION *gets it.*

MARION: Rock . . . Rock Hudson!

BENJAMIN: My turn, my turn . . .

    Young BENJAMIN *has done this before. He signals his hands to indicate a 'personality', Then he clears the air and begins to act.* TICK *is mesmerised. This is a remarkable child.* BENJAMIN *first mimes a woman, then makes a rocking motion with his arms, finally an animal. Everybody is stumped but* BERNADETTE, *who fills in the words to his mime.*

BERNADETTE: [*very drily*] Lindy Chamberlain. That was appalling, Benjamin. Who taught you that?

BENJAMIN: Mum did.

MARION: Lies. All lies.

BERNADETTE: I thought so. [*Getting to her feet.*] Come on Adam. Up.

ADAM climbs to his feet, a little embarrassed.
Time is against us and we have things to do.
She looks at TICK.
Come on, you butch thing you.
TICK: No. Count me out.
BERNADETTE: All for one.
ADAM: Come on, Tick.
TICK sits firm. He will not budge. BERNADETTE can see it will be hopeless. She pulls ADAM away.
BERNADETTE: Come on, Adam. Let's get frocked.

134. EXT. KINGS CANYON — LATE AFTERNOON

BENJAMIN is seated on a rock several hundred metres away from the picnic site. TICK is walking around, throwing the odd stone, struggling to find words.

TICK: So, what's it like to finally have a father?
BENJAMIN: It's OK.
Difficult silence.
TICK: Sorry about last night. I don't always dress up in women's clothes. I mean don't get the wrong idea. I do lots of different stuff . . . You know, like Elvis and Gary Glitter . . . and —
BENJAMIN: Abba?
TICK looks up startled.
I'm not supposed to know about the Abba show, but I'd really like to see it. Would you do Abba for me?
TICK is now lost for words. He eventually nods his head.
TICK: Sure. [*Gaining courage.*] You know what I am, don't you?
BENJAMIN: Mum says you're the best in the business.
TICK: [*flattered*] Well, your mother was always prone to exaggeration.
TICK suddenly realises what he is saying.
BENJAMIN: Will you have a boyfriend when we get back to Sydney?
TICK is stunned. It takes a long time to respond.
TICK: Maybe.
BENJAMIN: That's good.
A smile of relief begins to creep across TICK's face.

BENJAMIN catches on. The expression is returned. TICK grabs him by the hand and starts dragging him away.
TICK: Come on.
BENJAMIN: Where are we going?
TICK: We're going to unleash the best in the business.

135. EXT. KINGS CANYON — LATE AFTERNOON

At the base of Kings Canyon are three beautiful figures in full feathered drag, FELICIA, BERNADETTE and MITZI. There is a big climb ahead.

FELICIA: I had a dream.

MUSIC MONTAGE BEGINS

The ascension has begun. With a glorious sun dropping quickly behind, the three drag queens climb higher and higher. They are but spots on the face of the great red giant. The music is building. BERNADETTE is tiring. Her feet are killing her. MITZI is waving flies away with increasing weariness.
On the crescendo of a swelling score and with their feathers blowing in the wind, Mitzi Del Bra, Felicia Jollygoodfellow and Bernadette Bassinger arrive on the top of the world. They are dazzled.

MUSIC STALLS

136. EXT. KINGS CANYON/CRAG — SUNSET

The joy in FELICIA's face is beginning to subside. She looks across to the others who are taking in the enormity of the landscape all around them. A chilly wind is blowing the sun off the distant horizon.

FELICIA: Well, we did it.
    BERNADETTE scans the desert all around.
BERNADETTE: It never ends, does it? All that space.
    Silence.
FELICIA: So what now?
MITZI: I think I want to go home.

FELICIA: Me too.

> *BERNADETTE drops her hand and turns back to her companions. Their minds are made up. She lets out a sigh and smiles.*

BERNADETTE: Well then. Let's finish the shows and go home.

> *FELICIA and MITZI smile too.*

A FINAL FLOURISH OF MUSIC, THEN IT ENDS

137. ALICE HOTEL ENTRANCE — DAY

A few weeks have passed. 'Priscilla' is parked outside the foyer, ready to depart. BOB, dressed in a very smart hotel uniform, is throwing luggage into her side compartment. ADAM arrives, arms laden with the last of the baggage. The DOORMAN is very familiar.

DOORMAN: Don't go without giving me your number, Sunshine.

ADAM: Already taken care of, Jeff. It's at the far end of the men's cubicle. 'For a good time, phone Felicia.'

> *BENJAMIN is full of excitement.*

BENJAMIN: Hey. Can we stop at a McDonalds on the way back?

ADAM: Now that's a good idea. I've had just about enough of this shitty food. Fucking crayfish.

> *MARION and TICK walk around the side of the hotel towards the bus.*

TICK: I don't know. Where the hell do you start?

MARION: Oh stop it. Lay it on the line, husband. Don't conceal a thing. That's the key. And if he doesn't like it, stiff bikkies. He can always buy his own ticket back.

TICK: And what happens when word gets out that Mitzi's got a minor?

MARION: That's your problem, not his. He knows when and where to listen. Morals are a choice, and he'll decide his own when he's good and bloody well ready.

> *They all arrive at the back of the bus.*

BOB: That's it. You're all packed.

ADAM: You've got to be joking. We haven't got Bernadette's shoes on board yet.

BOB: Hate to say this, but I wish I was going with you. Your gas tank will be fine. Your axle may be another matter.

MARION: I'm sure the road home will be just filled with bored mechanics waiting for a bus full of drag queens to spirit them away to a better life.

TICK: I wish. We're not even going to spirit gum at this rate. Where the hell's Bernadette?

BERNADETTE: Here.

> *Everybody turns. BERNADETTE is standing with her hands clasped together, and a strange expression on her face.*

ADAM: Come on, cabanossi tits! Where are your bags?

BERNADETTE: In my room.

> *Silence. BOB very slowly walks over toward BERNADETTE, throwing her a supportive glance. TICK catches it. Something is up.*

BERNADETTE: I'm not going. I've decided to stay here for a while.

> *Absolute silence.*

TICK: Oh really. And you're choosing to tell us about this now.

MARION: She told me a few weeks back - just when I was looking for somebody to handle the guest entertainment while I'm away.

> *ADAM stares at BERNADETTE and then BOB.*

ADAM: Oh. I get it. Who's been playing hide the sausage then? That's it. Let's get out of here before I throw up. Come on Benj, hope you can drive.

> *ADAM climbs on board the bus with BENJAMIN, who is finding the whole thing great fun. TICK approaches the couple and stops. He looks to BOB, and then to BERNADETTE.*

TICK: Are you sure?

BERNADETTE: No, I'm not sure. But I'll never know unless I give it a shot.

> *TICK takes that in, and slowly puts his hands around his best girlfriend's shoulder. They hug for some time.*

TICK: I'm jealous as all hell.

> *BERNADETTE begins to cry.*

BERNADETTE: Shit. Raccoon time again.

MUSIC BEGINS

'Priscilla', pulling away from the hotel. TICK is waving out of the window. ADAM and BENJAMIN are leaning out of the back of the bus. BERNADETTE, BOB and MARION are all waving goodbye. Finally . . .

BENJAMIN: Bye, Ralph!
ADAM: Yeah, see you, Ralph!
    BERNADETTE's eyes narrow in fury.

138. INT. BUS — DAY

ADAM begins to mime to Abba's 'Mamma Mia', dancing down the aisle, with BENJAMIN in tow.

QUICK CUT TO . . .

139. INT. SYDNEY HOTEL — NIGHT

MUSIC CARRIES OVER

The familiar city hotel in which we first met the girls. It is full to capacity, the manic crowd going wild to the floor show by MITZI and FELICIA.
    The atmosphere is still as rough as ever, but the girls seem to be putting everything into the show.
    Sitting high on the shoulders of a man in the crowd is BENJAMIN, getting a bird's eye view of the festivities. And he is having a wonderful time. As the number draws to a close, the girls wind up, fall back for the finale and explode forward like we have never seen them do before.
    The mob lose control. The girls are pelted with plastic cups, beer, stray drinks and even the old faithful cans!
    Shielding herself from the debris, MITZI feels her way back to the D.J.'s desk, takes a microphone and turns to her adoring fans.

MITZI: That's enough. Oh, my tits are falling down. Thank you, thank you. It's good to be home.

FADE OUT. ROLL CREDITS

140. EXT. CHINESE MONASTERY GARDEN — DAY

A monk is walking in a garden when the drag kite lost in the desert skies many scenes earlier comes flying into his grasp. He examines her with great interest.

THE END

FILM CREDITS

POLYGRAM FILMED ENTERTAINMENT
IN ASSOCIATION WITH
THE AUSTRALIAN FILM FINANCE CORPORATION
PRESENTS A LATENT IMAGE/SPECIFIC FILMS
PRODUCTION

starring
TERENCE STAMP
HUGO WEAVING
GUY PEARCE
and BILL HUNTER

THE ADVENTURES OF PRISCILLA,
QUEEN OF THE DESERT

written and directed by
STEPHAN ELLIOTT

produced by
AL CLARK
MICHAEL HAMLYN

executive producer
REBEL PENFOLD-RUSSELL

POLYGRAM FILMED ENTERTAINMENT in association with THE AUSTRALIAN FILM FINANCE CORPORATION presents a LATENT IMAGE/SPECIFIC FILMS production
TERENCE STAMP HUGO WEAVING GUY PEARCE and BILL HUNTER "THE ADVENTURES OF PRISCILLA, QUEEN OF THE DESERT" production designer OWEN PATERSON
costume designers LIZZY GARDINER and TIM CHAPPEL film editor SUE BLAINEY director of photography BRIAN J BREHENY music by GUY GROSS executive producer REBEL PENFOLD-RUSSELL
MOVIE WB WORLD HOLLYWOOD ON THE GOLD COAST FFC Made with the participation of the Australian Film Finance Corporation Limited produced by AL CLARK and MICHAEL HAMLYN written and directed by STEPHAN ELLIOTT Produced with the assistance and financial participation of the NSW Film and Television Office polydor Soundtrack album available on Polydor Records
PolyGram ROADSHOW FILM DISTRIBUTORS DOLBY STEREO

Production Designer, Owen Paterson / Art Director, Colin Gibson / Costume Designers, Lizzy Gardiner and Tim Chappel / Film Editor, Sue Blainey / Music, Guy Gross / Director of Photography, Brian J Breheny / Executive Producer, Rebel Penfold-Russell / Producers, Al Clark and Michael Hamlyn / Writer and Director, Stephan Elliott

Associate Producer/Production Manager, Sue Seeary / First Assistant Director, Stuart Freeman / Production Accountant, John May / Production Co-ordinator, Esther Rodewald / Tyro Producer, Grant Lee / Assistant to Producer, Clare Wise / Second Assistant Directors, Emma Schofield and Maria Phillips / Third Assistant Director, Jamie Platt / Continuitywoman, Kate Dennis / Focus Puller, Adrien Seffrin / Clapper/Loader, Anna Townsend / 2nd Unit Camera, Martin Turner / 2nd Unit Assistant, Richard Bradshaw / 2nd Unit Co-ordinator, Grant Lee / Gaffer, Paul Booth / Best Naughty Boy, Matt Inglis / Third Electrics, Peter Holland / Key Grip, Pat Nash / Grip, Ian McAlpine / Grip's Assistant, Michael Gaffney / Sound Recordist, Guntis Sics / Additional Recording, Grant Shepherd / Boom Swinger, Fiona McBain / Key Make-up and Hair Artiste, Cassie Hanlon / Make-up/Hair, Angela Conte /Make-up and Hair/Drag Consultant, Strykermeyer / Wardrobe Supervisor, Emily Seresin / Wardrobe Co-ordinator, Brett Cooper / Designer's Assistant and Priest, Adam Dalli / Mr Breheny's Gowns by Miss 3D / Unit/Location Manager, Rick Kornaat / Unit Assistants, Russell Fewtrell, Paul Malane, Frank Mangano, Tim Duggan / Props Buyer, Kerrie Brown / Art Department Runner, Yann Dignes / Carpenters, Dougal Thompson, Jonathan Desprez / Welder, Lyall Beckmann / Prop Makers, John Murch, Philippa Playford / Art Dept Electrics, Graham Beatty / Soft Furnishings, Roz Hinde / Vehicle Coordinator and Wardrobe Modelling, Tim Parry / On-set Mechanics and Drivers, Mark McKinley, Peter Cogar / Choreographer, Mark White / Stunt Coordinator and Safety Supervisor, Robert Simper / Unit Nurse, Julia Gwilliam / Aerial Drag Pilot, Terry Lee / Stills Photographer, Elise Lockwood / Unit Publicity, Catherine Lavelle / Base Office Liaison, Kim Steblina / London Office Liaison, Jo O'Keefe / Tutor, Jenny-Lee Robinson / Tranny Trainer, Robyn Lee /

Catering, Marike's Catering Co. / Catering Assistants, Deb Gwilliam, Mark Nancarrow / Sunday Catering and Additional Direction, Colin Gibson / Big Cheese, Michael Kuhn / Additional Casting, Faith Martin and Assoc. / Broken Hill Casting, Bobbie Pickup, Quixote Casting / Coober Pedy Liaison, Dave Burge / **Cast in Order of Appearance** Tick/Mitzi, Hugo Weaving / Adam/Felicia, Guy Pearce / Bernadette, Terence Stamp / Logowoman, Rebel Russell / Bartender, John Casey / Shirley, June Marie Bennett / Miner, Murray Davies / Piano Player, Frank Cornelius / Petrol Station Attendant, Bob Boyce / Young Adam, Leighton Picken / Ma, Maria Kmet / Pa, Joseph Kmet / Aboriginal Man, Alan Dargin / Bob, Bill Hunter / Cynthia, Julia Cortez / Young Ralph, Daniel Kellie / Ralph's sister, Hannah Corbett / Ralph's father, Trevor Barrie / Frank, Ken Radley / Marion, Sarah Chadwick / Benjamin, Mark Holmes / **This space for rent: Your Name Here** / Post Production Supervisor, Sue Seeary / Post Production Liaison, Tony Lynch / Assistant Editor, Andy "Foofy" Yuncken / Telecine Operator, Michael Robertson / Title Design and Bad Acting, Libby Blainey / Post-production Facilities, Apocalypse / Mixed at Soundfirm Sydney / Digital Facilities, Philmsound / Sound supervised and mixed by Phil Judd / Additional Sound Design, Guntis Sics / Sound Co-ordinator/Effects Editor, Stephen "The Gherkin" Erskine / Assistant Effects Editor, Tim "Lobes" Colvin / Dialogue Editor, Angus "Goose" Robertson / ADR Recordist, Simon "Dionne" Hewitt / Foley Editors, Steve Burgess and Gerry Long / Foley recorded at Soundfirm Melbourne / Music recorded at Trackdown Studios / Music Engineer, Simon Leadley / Performed by Sydney Philharmonia Choir / Directed by Antony Walker / Soprano Solo by Robyn Dunn / Original Music published by Mushroom Music / Song Clearances, Diana Williams / Best Drag Queen Entrance, Russell Fewtrell / Film Stock, Kodak / Camera Equipment, Samuelson's / Camera Liaison, Bill Ross / Audio Equipment supplied by Audio Services Corporation Australia / Laboratory Facilities, Atlab Australia / Laboratory Liaison, Ian Russell / Colour Grading, Arthur Cambridge / Neg Matcher, Karen Psaltis / Legal Representation, Martin Cooper, Martin Cooper & Co. and Mark Devereux, Simon Olswang & Co. / Insurance

Broker, Lorraine Calway, Jardine Tolley / Completion Guarantor, Antonia Barnard, Film Finances Inc /Gloria's Puncture Kit provided by Owen Paterson / Make-up/Wardrobe Truck, Transfilm Location Services / Greenroom, Unit One Film Services / Helicopter, Professional Helicopter Services / Continental Mount, Continental Mounts Australia / Travel Co-ordination, Showtravel, Trudy Salven Travel Int'l / Freight Co-ordination, Traveltoo / **Extra Special Thanks (with cream on top):** Andrena Finlay, Peter Skillman / **Special Thanks (no cream, cherries optional)** Kim Green, Graham Bradstreet / **Quite Special Thanks (hold the sweetener)** Stewart Till, Aline Perry, Graeme Mason, Xavier Marchand and all at Manifesto, Kim Dalton, Ann Darrouzet, Keith Lupton, Maureen Barron, Tom Knapp, Billy Hinshelwood, Kathryn Smith, Jane Moore, Caroline Burton, Sarah Radclyffe, Martin Armiger, Tracey Mulligan, Brian Ross, David Cipriano, Sue Cohen / **Thanks also to** The South Australian Brewing Company Limited, Philips Consumer Electronics, Singer Australia Limited, Inchcape Liquor Marketing, M.M. Communications, Tracee Cosmetics, City Media, Wo-Man Beauty Products, Council of the City of Broken Hill, Broken Hill Regional Tourist Association, District Council of Coober Pedy, Conservation Commission of Northern Territory, Lasseters Hotel/Casino, Alice Springs, Mario's Palace Hotel/Motel, Australian Kite Flyers Society, Kings Canyon Resort / Map reproduced with permission of Gregory's Universal Press / International Sales Agent, Polygram Film Int'l / Film Gauge, 35mm Scope / Screen Ratio, 1:2.35. /Filmed entirely on location in New South Wales, South Australia and the Northern Territory in DRAGARAMA / Produced with the assistance and financial participation of the New South Wales Film and Television Office, Sydney, Australia.